ORIGINS
OF
DIFFERENCE

ORIGINS

OF

DIFFERENCE

The Gender Debate Revisited

Elaine Storkey

Baker Academic

A Division of Baker Book House Co
Grand Rapids, Michigan 49516

© 2001 by Elaine Storkey

Published by Baker Academic
a division of Baker Book House Company
P.O. Box 6287, Grand Rapids, MI 49516-6287

Printed in the United States of America

Library of Congress Cataloging-in-Publication Data

Storkey, Elaine, 1943–
    Origins of difference : the gender debate revisited / Elaine Storkey.
      p. cm.
    Includes bibliographical references and index.
    ISBN 0-8010-2260-6 (paper)
    1. Sex role. 2. Sex differences (Psychology) I. Title.
HQ1075.S78 2001
305.3—dc21   00-045423

For current information about all releases from Baker Book House, visit our web site:
http://www.bakerbooks.com

CONTENTS

PREFACE

n what ways are women and men really different, and where do the differences originate? These are probably two of the most common questions I have been asked during the years I have spent researching and lecturing on the issue of gender. It seems important to many people to know the answers, for if our differences are "fixed," part of our very biology, there is little we can do to alter them. (This is irrespective of whether that biology is seen as the last point in a process of evolution or given by a Creator.) We simply have to find a way of living with these differences creatively and in a way that produces minimum upset to the good ordering of our relationships. If, however, they are not fixed but are part of the shifts and changes in human fashion and social ideas, then we have much more flexibility. Once we have identified the pressures that shape gender differences, we can decide what to do about them. We can leave things as they are, or we can actively begin to reshape them.

A number of books deal with the issues of gender relationships, some of which have captured the popular imagination. Part of my own task has been to interact with these, but I have also tried to look more thoroughly at the questions that lie beneath many of their responses. My aim has been to question assumptions and challenge presuppositions, especially when those making them have taken them for granted.

In trying to present as cogently as possible complex arguments drawn from different academic disciplines, I have chosen a framework that I hope makes the material easy to follow. Each chapter takes the debate into a new area as the various strands of the discussion are identified. Chapter 1 sets the scene in historical context, chapters 2 through 4 handle the sociological and philosophical analysis, chapters 5 and 6 are psychological in focus, and chapters 7 through 9 concern theology. In chapter 10 I give my own brief response to the debate. There is an inevitable overlap, however, for my aim has been to discuss the issues that permeate the entire debate, rather than isolate the different academic disciplines.

Over the years that I have been involved in these issues, some positions have become untenable to me, and others seem much stronger. Inevitably, this means I will be sharing the way my own thinking has developed, which is, of course, why I have written this book. I recognize that heated disagreements often take place concerning this subject and that I may add fuel to the fire, although that is not my intention. While I offer a strong critique, I have tried to present the ideas of others as faithfully as I present my own.

This book is an edited, expanded, and updated form of the lectures I delivered to New College in the University of New South Wales in October 1997. In my writing I have taken into consideration many of the questions my audience at New College posed to me at that occasion as well as questions subsequent audiences presented. Not surprisingly, these have triggered more inquiries of my own. It has not been easy to write up the lectures for publication, for in this subject area the debate moves fast. In fact, a number of key studies were published as I was concluding my own work. Nevertheless, I have tried to incorporate as many of the new arguments and insights as I could, from the most recent material. I have also taken on board a particular point raised by one woman in Australia, after my lecture on gender differences in popular psychology. She commented that, although absorbing and entertaining, my lecture had not given her the critical analysis she was hoping for. I have worked hard to remedy that and hope chapters 5 and 6 will satisfy her request.

A revision of this extent means, however, that those who attended the lectures might find this account very different. They will miss the cartoons, the illustrations, and probably the jokes. Inevitably, lectures delivered to a group of colleagues and friends in the intimacy of an academic setting are different from a publication that tries to speak to a scattered audience many times the size. But I hope that those who heard the lectures think the finished product is an improvement and one that they are unashamed to hand out to their friends.

Some of the material in this book has a longer history than the New College Lectures, beginning life as notes for the London Lectures in Contemporary Christianity, which I delivered in London in 1993. These were reworked for the Jubilee Conference, an annual student gathering organized by the Pittsburgh Coalition for Christian Outreach. Throughout the 1990s, I visited a number of American colleges to address faculty and students, including trips to Calvin College, Michigan; Pittsburgh University Law School; Eastern College, Pennsylvania; Gordon-Conwell, Massachusetts; Allegheny College, Pennsylvania; Malone College, Ohio; and Penn State University. With this publication of *Origins of Difference*, I feel I have produced something that has been in the gestation stage for most of a decade. I am content, however, that it now addresses the current gender debate. Readers who are already familiar with the debate will find the material here complete in itself. Those who are less familiar will be helped by reading my first book, *What's Right with Feminism*. Published originally in 1985 and reprinted regularly, it has recently been updated in a new edition.

Acknowledgments

A s always, there are key people to thank. I am grateful for the invitation to deliver the original lectures, which was given by Dr. Allan Beavis, the Master of New College in Sydney. His hospitality, and that of all the colleges I visited, was rich and warm. I am in debt to Bishop John Reid, who first approached me with the idea, and to the New College Lectures Committee, who approved it. Fuzz and Carolyn Kitto of the Uniting Church in New South Wales were as hospitable as always and gave me practical and emotional support. Two colleagues at King's College, London, have been entirely supportive, Doug Campbell and Alan Torrance (now Professor of Divinity at St. Andrew's University, Scotland). Their own scholarship in theology has never ducked the issues raised by others I refer to in this book. Two of my graduate students in London, Celia McDonald and Clara Swinson, have produced material for me, along with Peter Oliver and Janet West in Sydney. Huw Spanner and Brian Draper of *Third Way* kept plying me with relevant books to consider (and of course to review!) as my own took shape. I am grateful to Catherine Clark Kroeger for suggesting an American edition of the book, to the development officer at Calvin College for his invitation to present the theme there, and to Peggar Dixon of the CCO in Pittsburgh for her invitation and support at the

Jubilee Conference. I also want to thank Robert Hosack and Melinda Van Engen of Baker Book House for seeing the manuscript through to publication. Finally, my husband, Alan, once again demonstrated that his commitment to gender equality is practical, not just romantic! He put up with my many absences as I delivered the lectures and my inaccessibility in the home as I worked on the manuscript. To him and to everyone I offer grateful thanks.

HISTORY LESSONS

or those who like order, predictability, and a settled way of doing things, the 1950s now seem like a period of unparalleled bliss. The war had ended, American servicemen had come home to enjoy family life, and a sober optimism had settled over Europe. Politically, people were jubilant. Fascism had been wiped out, communism seemed for the moment to be at bay, and good had triumphed over evil. Of course, there were things to be sorted out. Some writers wrote solemnly of the "profound crisis of man,"[1] and full awareness of the extent of the atrocities that took place during the war was still dawning. A report issued in 1945 by the inspectors sent from the allied nations to Buchenwald—the Jewish extermination camp—makes for chilling reading. They documented the horrors—trenches full of corpses, furniture and lampshades in the commandant's house made from human skin—but said they had no evidence of any actual torture. Jewish survivors told them of camps they believed were worse. The inspectors reported simply, "The name of Auschwitz occurred several times."

By the 1950s, we knew all about Auschwitz and much more. Yet, there was little counseling for either the returned war veterans or for the devastated Jewish community, so many of whom had seen their families decimated. All the men and women damaged by the war simply had to put it behind them and plan for the future. The world was committed to peace, to prosperity, to rebuilding for the future, and to change. In the United States, the population leaped to 150 million, 20 million more than in the previous decade. As one American put it, after the war, people wanted children, and "every woman, and her sister, was having a baby."[2] In Britain, my parents' generation slowly rebuilt our country and tried, like people throughout Europe, to return to normality. For some, that return was not to be, and the search for a new start drew many families from England to Canada, Australia, and New Zealand. There they began a different life with different challenges, although content for the next few decades to be joined with the old country under its new young monarch, who had succeeded to the throne. In spite of all we had been through, the mood everywhere was cautiously optimistic. Britain witnessed an end to rationing, an availability of jobs for everyone, and a massive reconstruction problem that needed to be tackled: the rebuilding of lives, cities, the economy, schools, universities, and families.

The problem was, however, that it was never that simple, for the war had unsettled relationships and challenged patterns of hierarchy and values. The 1950s ultimately failed to win the new generation over to the perspectives of the old. Things were changing at the very heart of these societies. One key change involved how men and women were to relate to each other in the varied tasks of postwar life. Issues of sex and gender began to surface in the areas of work, education, marriage, and family, with modifications taking place that many in society did not understand. Why could things not stay as they were? But as they were when? During what period of time? There were historical variants in the relationships between men and women, and in so many ways, this new half century was to be quite unlike any that had gone before. Who was to say which of the historical patterns of relating needed to be called upon and adhered to in the years following the 1950s?

Analyzing the past was not, however, the usual method chosen for sorting out issues of sex and gender, for, strange though it might now seem, people in the 1950s were largely unaware of gender history. Most of it was not written up until over a decade later. The relevant stories in that history had not been the focus of university research or programs of teaching. Memories were tossed around in folklore or old family archives but were not fully recorded and studied in public places. Even recent gender history—say that of American women in the nineteenth century—was often inaccessible, unless people went looking for it. Many fascinating accounts of why European women emigrated from the 1800s onward, especially from Britain to Australia and New Zealand, were not yet available. We had to wait two decades or more before excited students of history finally wrote these accounts.[3]

A Hidden History of Nineteenth-Century Women

This absence of analysis is curious because, even though it had rarely been articulated self-consciously in history books, the United States and Britain had struggled with the gender issue over and over again. Many aspects of that struggle had taken place in the nineteenth century, which, for people in the 1950s, was still recent or even living memory. There were of course the big public issues, which had resulted in constitutional change in America. Both emancipation and women's suffrage had been campaigns spearheaded initially by women, and these certainly were known to have mounted a major challenge to gendered ways of thinking. But hundreds of less well-documented issues also marked American life throughout the nineteenth century, covering every area from temperance to childbirth practices to theology, and often involving very colorful women.

We could take, as an example, the Anti-Saloon League. This considerable movement of women campaigned against the alcohol racket and the level of alcohol consumption among men because of the devastating effects drinking had on wives and children. These women challenged the regime of "boss rule," in which the bosses who paid the workers received back the wages they had paid through the drinking and gambling saloons, leaving families subject to poverty and violence. In some areas, League women marched on the saloons with a Bible in one hand and a hatchet in the other, urging the barman to pour his whisky on the ground. If the sermon did not prevail, the ax would!

Many other examples could help to show that the issue of gender had been alive and well in America for over a century, even though few people in the 1950s were reflecting on it. Certainly, none of this was regarded as vital curriculum material for the history programs in schools and colleges. It was not taught constructively in churches or Sunday school classes. The details were preserved largely through old photographs, yellowed newspaper articles, and folk memory handed down through families.

There had also been issues in Britain in the nineteenth century that were now largely disregarded. One was the old problem of the "superfluous woman." In the 1860s and again in the 1880s, for example, many men were killed in wars, leaving an imbalance in the adult population. Demographic factors added to this, for the infant mortality rate was higher among young male infants. Consequently, for much of the latter part of the nineteenth century, there was an acute problem of too few men and too many women in the British population, a problem that would worsen after World War I.

How did we learn of this? Again, not through history classes in the 1950s but through the legacy of party games. The Victorians had an intriguing card game called "Old Maid," which involved collecting cards of family members, mother, father, son, daughter, and so on, until one had a full set. But also in the pack was the one card nobody wanted, namely, the "Old Maid." The point of the game was to use any amount of ingenuity or deceit to get rid of the Old Maid from your hand of acceptable family relations by palming her off on someone else. In humorous, yet cruel, detail, this game echoed the problem of the "superfluous woman" in British society. An unmarried middle-class woman was a liability. Working-class women could go into domestic service or factory work, but a lady too highly bred for such labor was always someone's dependent: a father's, uncle's, or brother's.

It is interesting to note the various solutions to this problem that society found. Family members could marry her off, send her out as a governess or companion to an elderly widow, encourage her to join one of the newly revitalized religious orders, or ship her off to the Colonies. Hundreds of unmarried ladies took this final option and crossed the ocean. The English Gentlewoman's Emigration Society, founded by an Anglican clergyman, offered a relatively protected passage for single travelers and provided spunky middle-class women as wives for the farmers and workers of Australia and New Zealand, where there was still a woman shortage. The very first settlement at Botany Bay had been overwhelmingly male. Out of 725 convicts, only 192 were women. Half a century later men still predominated. Once the women were there, of course, they worked. Gentlewomen who, in Britain, would have been barely able to move across the room, so tightly were they laced into their waist-pinching "waspies," hacked into the native bush, worked as ranchers' wives, or traveled long distances on horseback. Some thrived on the change and discovered a freedom of space and basic lifestyle completely unavailable to them in Britain. Yet, for others it cannot have been an easy life, especially when expatriate gentlewomen were an oddity in the society. As Janet West remarks in her excellent study, the cult of machismo in Australia is "probably a descendent of the early colonial days of womanlessness."[4] How the emigrant women coped is a major study of its own.

WOMEN'S EDUCATION

Marked changes in other areas of women's lives had taken place in the nineteenth century as well. High on the list was education. In every era of European history, there had been those parents who had believed that an educated woman is a better companion than an uneducated one and had provided tutors for their daughters. But women's education became public policy in the nineteenth century, extending into higher education. Coeducational education was early on the scene in America. Oberlin College opened in Ohio in 1833, and Antioch College, in the same state, followed twenty years later. In fact, beyond the Mississippi, every state university, except that of Missouri, was coeducational from the start. In other places, exceptional women were sometimes admitted for studies. Elizabeth Blackwell gained entrance to the Geneva Medical School in 1847, and despite difficulties of being accepted by her colleagues, graduated at the head of her class in 1849. In 1865, Vassar became the first bona fide women's college, but the oldest universities were more resistant to change. Harvard University, founded in 1636, enrolled no women until Elizabeth Agassiz helped to open the Harvard Annex, specifically for them, in 1879. In 1894, this annex became Radcliffe College, with Agassiz, fittingly, as its first president. With the establishment of Smith and Wellesley in 1875 and Bryn Mawr in 1885, women were now studying on equal terms with men.[5]

British education was similarly on the move. Girton in Cambridge (initially known as Hitchin College), founded in 1869, was the first women's residential college (a mere 585 years after Peterhouse, the first Cambridge men's college founded in 1284!). Although Cambridge did not actually allow women to be *equal* members of the university for another eighty years, the University of London opened degrees to women in 1878. By the turn of the century, therefore, women were accepted as at least a peripheral part of the undergraduate world. In 1897, the Women's Institute produced a listing of women at each university in Britain. The nine women's colleges of Cambridge, Oxford, and London Universities had a total of 778 students, the largest number (192) being admitted to Bedford College, London, which had opened in 1849. The London residential college, Westfield, founded on Evangelical Church of England principles with Bible study at the center of its curriculum, had forty-four women on its list.[6]

Finally, in Australia and New Zealand a similar pattern followed. Compulsory education for both sexes had been introduced from 1866 onward. Victoria implemented this in 1874, South Australia in 1875, and New South Wales in 1880. The University of Adelaide opened in 1872 and allowed women to attend lectures from the start, but they could not receive degrees until 1880. It took nine years of planning and negotiation before Melbourne opened its university to women, and that was not until Sydney University had declared the principle of women's rights and equality in 1888.[7] Women had been given the rights to higher education in New Zealand in 1870.

It was evident, then, that women's education had been slowly gaining ground throughout the English-speaking world. The result was that by the beginning of the twentieth century the possibility of professional employment for women was beginning to look like an attractive alternative to economic dependence on male relatives. For some women it was an attractive alternative even to marriage.

MISSIONARY WORK

The growth in women's education brought what appeared to be vocational benefits to Christian women. Now, in principle at least, they could be better equipped educationally for the work of Christian ministry and take their place alongside men as educated teachers and preachers in congregations. Unfortunately, this did not happen. For the most part, little significant change in women's leadership took place across the spectrum of American churches. In fact, there had been wider acceptance of women preachers earlier in the century. Certainly, several key figures such as Phoebe Palmer, Lucretia Mott, and Sojourner Truth were well known as women gifted in preaching. But these were still the exceptions. It would take more than qualifications in higher education before women would be widely accepted as leaders of American congregations.

The same was true in Britain. Christian women who felt a call to evangelize had to travel overseas. So travel they did, and on journeys that sometimes took weeks. The nineteenth century saw an outpouring of women's talents into foreign climes. Unlike some of the other women we noted, however, these women did not go to find basic employment or a husband; they went to give their lives to missionary activity in far distant lands. Not surprisingly, therefore, overseas missions made great use of women right from the start.

The Society for Promoting Female Education in the Far East had begun in the late 1820s, and early missionaries set up five schools in Malacca. In India the Zenana Bible and Medical Mission, founded in the 1850s, was a women's mission for over a hundred years before admitting men as members in 1952. The year 1877 marked a turning point for women missionaries in China as a famine in the Shansi province claimed the lives of nine to thirteen million people and opened doors to Western women to work and minister to those who survived.[8] Mary Lawry was the first missionary born in Australia to serve overseas. She went out from Parramatta with her English-born husband to Tonga and worked with the Tongans on their own ground, visiting them in their homes. (Her ministry was markedly more successful than her husband's, but this did not stop the Wesleyan Methodist magazine from editing her name out of her husband's accounts of their work in Tonga.)[9]

19

Whether in Calabar or in the Crimea, much of this early work was undertaken in uncharted territory where few westerners had ever been before. And it was carried out often without backup from organized agencies that could offer support and sometimes protection. Long before the later missionary societies had devised programs of preparation for overseas missionary work, these early women learned the local language and customs for themselves and gave a lifetime of service to cultures they had made their own. How they coped with homesickness and frustration is the subject of many poignant biographies.

SUFFRAGE

A third key area for women was their involvement in political democracy. The suffrage campaigns were especially significant. Both New Zealand and Australia made much earlier progress than America or Britain. In New Zealand in 1893, thirteen years after women had received the right to a tertiary education in the country's universities, they were given the right to vote. This was not without opposition of course; the campaigners had been parodied as the "shrieking sisterhood." A year later, 1894, women were given the vote in South Australia. The Woman's Suffrage League had persuaded almost one-third of the colony's adult population to sign a petition calling for universal suffrage. South Australia also became the first place in the world to allow women to run for the legislature. In Canada, women waited until 1918, and in America they waited until 1920 to vote in federal elections. Not until 1928 did Britain grant suffrage to all women over 21.

The suffrage campaign in Britain, however, had undoubtedly been held up by the First World War, whose aftermath brought another massive demographic problem. Thousands of women lost their husbands, fiancés, and sweethearts and were never to marry again. It is no coincidence that the 1920s in Britain saw an upsurge in spiritualist interest among women as they tried to contact the dead. But, more usefully, it also saw the burgeoning of new openings for women in the professions, the final key area of change for women. Certainly, women were now educated for these roles, but there was also the necessity of ordering a society in a way that did not require equal numbers of marriageable men and women in the population. Consequently, the growth in women's education, the opening up of the professions, and the acceptance that a single woman no longer had to be economically dependent on her male relatives all helped women break into areas of work that had previously been the sole preserve of men. Hardy women professionals created a new tradition alongside the old-boy networks and passed on their skills to younger women. By the outbreak of the Second World War, women knew what would be expected of them. Many of them were ready to move into the areas of economic planning and production vacated by the men at the front.

REACTIONS IN THE 1950s

Long before the 1950s, therefore, the gender issue had surfaced again and again. Questions that involved the relationships of women and men were constantly on the agenda and were responded to in many varied ways. Considering how much ground had been covered, it still remains strange that those cameos of recent history were so disregarded in the 1950s. It was almost as though the postwar mind could not take in too much subtlety, could not cope with too many variations after all it had gone through. For whatever reasons, the fifteen years after the Second World War were a period of unparalleled "traditionalism." The men demobilized from the armed forces needed work, the countries needed children, and families needed mothers. It was a time when stability was prized almost above all else.

In Britain, although less so in the United States, the return to domesticity went largely uncontested. The role of homemaker, which continued long after children had left home, was experienced as liberation for those who had been required to go to work during the war. And so the emphasis on the male breadwinner was reinforced by the media, schools, and public policies. Education programs made some nod toward the need to equip women for dual careers of motherhood and work, but by and large work was seen along strong lines of gender demarcation. Gender history was put on hold, and those who were Christianly inclined saw those roles as laid down by God.

Yet, the status quo would not hold for long. The assumption that an unbroken line of fixed sex and gender roles extended from the Garden of Eden to the middle of the twentieth century was soon going to be shattered. A new generation in Britain that had not embraced the need for sacrifice for king and country was going to call into question all that the 1950s stood for. It was going to challenge politics, economics, sexuality, education, morality. It was going to join the wave of unrest in the United States and rethink the traditions of its forebears as simply "conservative ideology." And the debate about sex and gender was going to be one of the most turbulent debates of all.

PREMODERN, MODERN, AND POSTMODERN

I have chosen to position my comments around the 1950s because that period is now sometimes regarded as the last era in which public attitudes were consensual and largely "premodern." It is becoming commonplace among some contemporary writers to distinguish between the "premodern," "modern" and "postmodern,"[10] and I want to borrow those categories now. I do so, however, recognizing that this classification has limitations, for these three terms are not very precise analytical tools. There are no specific epochs or dates that these categories refer to, for they are not historical groupings. Nor do they describe social movements or rigorous intellectual schools of thought. They are more nebulous: concepts that relate to cultural demarcations, mind-sets, attitudes, value systems.

The "premodern," which embraces many of the attitudes widespread in the 1950s, is about predictability and tradition and is markedly different from the "modern" and its questioning of ideology and its identification of hidden assumptions. With an emphasis on competing explanations and consciousness-raising, the modern challenged the premodern but replaced traditional values with an ideology of its own, which in turn has been rejected. Since the mid-1980s, we have been moving into the "postmodern," which recognizes, most of all, the fluidity of relationships, the plurality of cultures, the diversity of people groups, the dethroning of the West and Western ideology, and the relativism of meanings. Of course, it is in the very nature of postmodernity that it does not exist on its own. In our postmodern society there will be very many (often the majority) who are still premodern and modern. But culturally their voice will be muted and their relevance often dismissed because they belong to another era: something more fixed, more definite, appealing to a metanarrative.

In working with these demarcations, I recognize that my comments will be provisional, but that is in keeping with the postmodern, for in postmodernity there are few endings and no fixed points of reference. Yet, my own analysis is not a postmodern one. It has not rejected the possibility of a comprehensive framework of understanding. Certainly, it is one that recognizes the importance of "deconstruction" and yet also acknowledges that we can only deconstruct from a particular location. My own location will become evident as the chapters unfold.

Although I have said that the 1950s are regarded as the last era when public attitudes were premodern, this does not mean that premodernity no longer exists except among individual people. In fact, with regard to the relationship between men and women, those attitudes have continued to exist in substantial pockets of society, whatever else has changed in the way we see things. The very question of this book, whether as human beings, male and female, we are "created or constructed"—whether our human sexual identity is mapped out by our place in some "natural order" or is shaped by our social context—has not been settled during any period. The debate has been continuous. Even when the overall cultural response has gone in one direction, there have always been substantial influential minorities that have taken up a different answer. I now want to examine the debate about sex and gender relations in light of the demarcations of premodern, modern, and postmodern. I believe that what sounds provisional at the outset will be much firmer by the conclusion.

23

THE PREMODERN IN SEX AND GENDER

W hen I decided to borrow the concepts of premodern, modern, and postmodern, I inherited a problem. Whose definition do I use? In fact, the answer has already been decided, for these concepts are those developed by postmodern writers. In other words, the premodern, for example, does not actually exist except as a category offered to us by postmodernity. So to use these terms at all means I initially have to allow the postmodern definitions to prevail. What follows in this chapter is therefore an analysis already filtered through a certain value framework. I shall reappraise this later, but meanwhile, readers can assess for themselves to what extent the analysis holds weight.

According to Jean Joseph Goux, the premodern is characterized by fixed order, fixed roles, and fixed explanations, reinforced by accepted tradition.[1] At its heart lies an essentialism, the idea that a certain "essence" defines the center of our identity as human beings and as men and women. In gender terms this means that men have certain identifiable, fixed characteristics, and women have other identifiable, fixed characteristics, and that these identifiers are rooted in our very nature. Whether this is backed by careful analysis or serious scholarship has not mattered until recently. The appeal has always been to what is supposedly obvious and needs no explanation.

Premodern thinking about gender relations, if indeed it can be given the label "thinking," was therefore largely at the level of assumption rather than analysis or examination. Attitudes about men and women, epitomized in the 1950s, were widely held but rarely scrutinized or reflected on. Even so, these attitudes undergirded much of society. They were reflected in family patterns, work roles, social policy, and curriculum development. They were reinforced by advertising, films, and romantic novels. Men were always tall, strong, direct, and authoritative; women were always passive, responsive, attractive, and young. The romantic, Hollywood fantasy was that the ultimate success of a woman was in transforming one of these male creatures from a single-minded, focused decision maker into a hopelessly lovelorn suitor who thought of little else but her.

The gender attitudes of premodernity became "normalized" in the minds of those who expressed them. These attitudes defined reality, and it took another era to identify them as ideological. Well-worn clichés and strings of truisms justified most social practices, if indeed any justification was deemed necessary. A woman's place was in the home. Women were intuitive, nurturant, passive, instinctual, emotional, good with their fingers, but easily distracted. As "weaker vessels" women needed to be protected, often from themselves and their own irrationality. Men were the ones to whom this task of leadership and protection automatically fell. They were strong, protective, hardy, analytical, objective, and more single-minded. Men were best suited to lead, women to follow. Men, with their greater rational, objective capacity could more readily detach themselves from emotional situations, whereas women were too easily influenced by their feelings.

The societies that were built on these attitudes were inevitably ones that prized and rewarded characteristics seen as male: toughness, inflexibility, hard bargaining, single-minded vision, uncompromising firmness, confrontation and defeat of opponents. Not surprisingly, in this masculine-constructed reality (what later feminists would call patri-archy), those men who found themselves ill at ease with these stereo-types courted disapproval and felt excluded.

There were ways "real" men could express love for each other, but these were stereotypical and culturally closed. They were evident in the "buddiness" of the American hunting-shooting-fishing fraternity, symbolized by Robert Bly in *Iron John,* or in the restrained stiff-upper-lip emotions of the English officer class. True depth of feeling was rarely betrayed by language. "I just want to say, sir, you are a fine leader and a very decent chap, and I would give my life for you." While women were given permission to express a wide range of passions to each other, men struggled to find their own language of feelings within emotionally repressive cultures. Insults, thumping, practical jokes, heavy drinking, and general bawdiness were the vehicle in Australian machismo gatherings. The message conveyed, subtly but unmistak-ably, was that for men to display any emotion other than loyalty, pride at achievement, competitiveness, anger, or controlled lust was unmanly. If in their relationship with women the control was not always there, that was also understandable.

How did the premodern mind justify its stereotypes? Almost always by an appeal to what was called the "natural," usually identified as bio-logical and frequently as God-given. Human attributes were all cre-ated, or, for those who had no time for a Creator, they evolved. Male and female characteristics were fixed, rooted in nature, in biology. They were "givens," indelible, nonnegotiable imperatives, and formed the basis for all human authority structures. The forces of biology were definitive and unchanging. For either sex to move away from their given characteristics and adopt those that pertained to the opposite sex was alarming. Such a move went against nature. Certain branches of the church claimed to find a reinforcement of this essentialism in biblical teaching, insisting that it is implied in the very order of cre-ation. Since nature was created by God, and since it was God's idea to have male and female, the blurring of sexual distinctiveness must surely transgress the very will of God. Something that was called "nat-ural order" or "tradition as divinely ordained" had to be fiercely upheld.

The French writer Fénelon expressed in 1721 what many premod-erns were to maintain for the next two and a half centuries: "To vio-

27

late the rights of established subordination is . . . to blaspheme against Providence, and threaten the rights of the sovereign father and head of the family who gives to each of his children his allotted place."[2] To alter established gender roles was nothing less than to desex humanity. As we shall see later, these attitudes were still evident in the 1990s in the Church of England debate on the ordination of women, and in the reemergence of evangelical patriarchy in some parts of the United States.

What became evident is that for those who thought in a premodern way, the sex-gender dichotomy did not exist. There was no difference between sex and gender, for all was decided by sex. Biology provided the essentialism that delivered the structure of all human roles and relationships. The idea that there were cultural reasons for the way men and women functioned was not seriously considered. The splitting apart of "sex" as a biological category and "gender" as a cultural category had to wait until the modern writers began their critique.

The main problem with the premodern position is now well recognized. It rests on a biological determinism that reduces all the complexity of human relationships to basic genetic or anatomic categories. Like all reductionist positions, it shrinks reality. Yet, premodern assumptions have never disappeared from the gender debate, and indeed, they have been making something of a comeback in recent years. Because of this, and indeed as a matter of common courtesy, we need to pay some attention to the arguments that place much weight on biology. We need to examine, too, the anxieties about changing roles that are often evident among traditionalists, including Christians, who hold this position.

The Evidence from Biology

It would be foolish to deny that biology plays a key part in human relationships and sexual differentiation. Men and women are not only sexually different, they are different chromosomally, reproductively, anatomically, hormonally, and in terms of weight, height, and brain usage. Figures quoted suggest that men are, on average, 7 percent taller and 20 percent heavier than women. The very categories—male and female—are *sexual* categories, and we experience much of our identity through our sexuality. What is more, premodern notions about what is natural did not emerge from nowhere. They were often rein-forced by research from psychologists or biologists. Studies on the effects of an "explosion of testosterone" in aggressive behavior in male rats may be dated and rather dubious when applied directly to male humans, but clearly there is something of consequence that needs to be taken into consideration. Similarly, although far too much has been laid at the door of "premenstrual tension," it also has some signifi-cance. Women's mood swings and attitudes toward events, work, or relationships are not dissociated from their biological cycle.

Longevity

The differences between men and women express themselves in other evident ways. Of the current population in Britain, fewer than 1.1 million people live to be over 85 years of age. But among those aged 89, there are three women to every man.[3] A similar difference exists in most of the United States. The conclusion is unavoidable. Put simply, women last longer. And this is in spite of childbearing and the increase of invasive cancers among women. Some argue that women face fewer hazards than men do, that men take on the more danger-ous tasks that reduce their life expectancy. Yet, studies comparing sur-vival rates among males and females with similar lifestyles suggest there are other factors.

An interesting piece of research was done some years ago on forty thousand monks and nuns. This was a very useful comparative sam-ple, for both groups were free from the perils of dangerous occupa-tions, from emotional traumas of family life, and from normal work stresses. Moreover, they were all nonsmokers and teetotalers. If any group could be expected to show a similarity in life expectation, it should be this one. Yet, the study established that by the age of 45, the nuns could expect to live five and a half years longer than the monks![4] Biological differences obviously play some part.

Sexual Disorders

The influence of biology comes out even more strongly when we look at the effects of sexual disorders in men and women. For exam-

29

ple, the disorder S alpha–reductese deficiency (an enzyme deficiency), results in genetic males being born with genitalia of female appearance. Therefore, there is an ambiguity about sexuality until puberty, when, with the usual surge of testosterone, masculinity occurs—the voice deepens and the phallus enlarges. Problems of coping with the disorder are often compounded because many of these young men have previously been raised as girls. Whatever problems of sexual identity these particular young people have already encountered will be much greater after puberty, as they now have to learn the behavior, patterns, and attitudes of men. The counter disorder in women, congenital adrenal hyperplasia, is a genetically recessive condition that leads to virilization of females—i.e., genetically female children are born with masculinized genitalia, again corresponding with a resultant confusion of identity. There is also some evidence of an increased incidence of lesbianism in women with this disorder. The conclusions from these observations are that biology is a powerful determinant of our identity, and when biology sends ambiguous messages, people are thrown into confusion.[5]

Brain Hemispheres

Yet, however significant hormonal influence or sexual disorders may be (and they are obviously very significant in the lives of those who have to work through them), some people place too much weight on them when making their overall argument about male-female differences. That is why some others who argue for biology make their case, more enthusiastically, from research done on male-female brains and the contrasting usage by men and women of different brain hemispheres. A number of claims have been made. "The difference between the male and female brain is now well attested by different researchers. Women have stronger connections between the two halves of their brains, men have stronger connections within each half of the brain." Or, put another way, "Women have the skills to win the Nobel Peace Prize, but it is a rare woman who will win the Nobel Prize for Physics or for Economics, and that has nothing to do with society's bias, but all to do with the male's inbuilt advantage. He simply finds higher or abstract mathematics easier."[6] Some have taken these points so seriously that they suggest it is not only inefficient and wasteful to train women to think "like men," it might also be harmful.[7]

Sociobiology

It is interesting that there has been a comfortable alliance between those who hold to the position that a natural order is established by biology and premoderns whose starting point is Christianity. I shall focus more on this later, but here I want to say that Christians who believe that different sex roles are willed by God and reinforced by Scripture are pleased to see their ideas given some "scientific" weight. Yet, although they find some of these theories relatively benign, other theories from the same stable are clearly problematic. Christians with "biologistic" sympathies do not know what to make of sociobiology, for example. On the one hand, it stresses the gulf between male and female more than any other theory. On the other, it rests so heavily on an aggressive evolutionary base and produces an ethical standpoint that is at best amoral and at worse the law of the jungle. I have attended lectures at which I have witnessed a great deal of enthusiasm for the categorical nature of the assertions, until the implications for moral judgments are pointed out.

Sociobiology attempts to explain the origins of differences between male and female behavior. It also tries to address what effect biology has on the structuring of societies. Unlike the other research already discussed, the focus here is not anatomy, hormones, physiology, or brain hemispheres. It is the *gene*. Through gene information, traits and characteristics are passed from one generation to the next. The "selfish gene theory" in effect argues that one of the most basic genetic impulses throughout all species is the desire to reproduce. Therefore, we are driven to find the maximal conditions to ensure the survival of *our* genes, even if that means the destruction of others. And this gives us the clue to male-female roles and behavior patterns.

Men and women have different amounts of reproductive material. Men produce sperm in extremely large quantities. Women have eggs in relatively small numbers, and because of the period of gestation, not even all of these could produce babies. In practice, then, a man could produce hundreds of offspring if he could find enough sexual partners

31

and summon up enough energy. Yet, if a woman managed to give birth to twenty children, she would be doing very well! So at the heart of our difference lies this genetic diversity—men have many more chances than women of reproducing their genes. And, say the sociobiologists, conflict is inevitable, because the needs of each sex are so different. Men need many partners and are genetically driven toward promiscuity and competitiveness. Women, on the other hand, need a protected environment. They need security and the best mate possible to ensure the maximum efficiency and survival of their genes. Their "drives," therefore, are toward exclusiveness and stability. Now, societies do what they can to organize themselves so that these incompatible needs can best be met. But what are seen as societal disorders—rape and male violence—is the spillover of the genetic differences between male and female. These reemerge spasmodically and inevitably, resisting the social taboos that we have used to restrain them.

Not surprisingly, given all the examples offered above, the tendency to root all differences between women and men ultimately in biology (whether seen as created by God or as a product of evolution) has proven powerful. What other source can there be? The onus has been on those who disagree to offer a better explanation.

Problems with These Explanations

Although apparently persuasive, problems exist with each of these explanations. Sociobiology[8] has glaring weaknesses in that it has no basis for any coherent moral framework. When everything is referred back to the need to procreate, what sexual ethic is possible except "follow your urges"? That has made it less attractive to many who might otherwise have supported it. It is difficult to justify buying into a theory that by implication justifies rape and promiscuity! Other critics point out that a strictly biological explanation also rests on a variety of concepts that are highly speculative, such as "genetic predispositions" or "the selfish gene." Although the hypothesis claims to rest on empirical science, how can you ever devise a means of testing it? The theory also uses a dubious methodology of induction from animal research to human motivation. Yet, it is not only sociobiology that is problematic. All of these positions, which rest on assumptions about the inevitability of our biology, have fundamental flaws, for any reductionism offers a weak theoretical framework. Social, cultural, and psychological factors, which are complex in nature, cannot be reduced to biological ones. Even when we look at uncontrovertible evidence from examples of sexual disorder, biology is not the full story. Being told you are a girl, while you are born with male genitalia, is also going to cause gender confusion. It will involve one's sense of self and one's relationships with parents, peers, siblings, and members of the opposite sex. Reinforcement of gender attitudes over many years are much more difficult to undo than learning to adopt a different position from which to urinate!

There is also an underlying problem here with definitions. Very often the concepts we use are defined in a way that assumes the "male is norm." Look at the word *strength* for example. It usually refers to muscle power, vigor, force, ability to lift weights, and so on. Within this definition the obvious conclusion is that men are stronger than women. They run faster, throw farther, hit harder. But if we changed the definition to include stamina, perseverance, or the longevity we noted earlier, we would have a different paradigm. Then, women would be as strong as men, if not stronger, since they stay alive longer and can carry babies within their bodies for nine months. Our definitions do more than just denote difference; they evaluate it along male lines.

How far all these classifications take us is dubious anyway. Take the studies on male-female differences in the way we use our brains. It is full of ambiguities. The Nobel Prize–winner neuroscientist Roger Sperry has warned against the tendency to go too far in connecting certain abilities to each side of the brain, pointing out how much more the brain works as an integrated whole.[9] Since his own work is on hemispheric specialization, that is advice worth heeding. At the safest level of conclusion it would seem that women are more likely to use the parts of their brain that develop linguistic skills, whereas boys develop the skills that take them into science or engineering. However, that fact alone does not help us much. A contemporary researcher suggests that if you translate this into what happens in jobs in society, it would produce a ratio of 3:2 of men to women. That means we could expect 60 percent of all scientists and engineers to be male and

40 percent female. But nothing like 40 percent of scientists and engineers are female. The ratio is much smaller. In fact, for the last thirty years more than 90 percent of engineers have been men. The findings from research into male and female brains, therefore, do not explain the disparity that has actually existed. Nor do they explain the other changes today, such as the fact that girls in the United Kingdom are beginning to outdo boys educationally in most subjects, including the sciences, and are beating them at all levels of the educational system. In the year 2000, girls' examination results surpassed those of boys at all levels of school education. Even in physics, the male predominance was challenged.

These issues are not just about biology, therefore, for clearly something more than biology is at stake. Nor are they simply about what is "natural" because what one society thinks is "natural" another society can think is highly "unnatural." What has been missing from the equation is a recognition of the social framework—the location, upbringing, expectations, and belief structures that people hold—for these factors give shape to our ideas about sex and gender and translate those ideas into action. We can see it in our story of history. As we moved out of the first half of the twentieth century, ideas began to change, and practices and social patterns slowly followed. This awareness of cultural pressures and a reflection on the part they play became very important to those thinkers who were about to follow.

34

The early postwar period of the "return to normality" was coming to a close. The optimistic rebuilding of the 1950s and the traditional assumptions about sex were to be shaken by an unprecedented storm of radicalism in the 1960s. Modernist analyses of gender were about to attack premodernity at its very foundations and frame a new structure on the edifice of the old. In particular, the assumptions about the limitations of biology were going to be seen in the light of political and social constructions. Education, equal pay legislation, and a shift in the composition of the workforce would force a tense rethinking. The debate about male and female was about to enter a dramatic new phase.

Modernism and Gender Relationships

t is somewhat banal to refer to the social theorists writing in the 1960s and 1970s simply as "modernists." Theirs were complex arguments, and there were many differences and disagreements between them. But I want to adopt the term *modernist* in the way it is used by postmodern writer Jean Joseph Goux to denote the middle point of a journey between premodernity and post-modernity.[1] I want to suggest it was the modernists who moved the gender debate from a focus on creation to construction. In Goux's analysis, they did this because their central concern was a rebellion against biological essentialism.

This rebellion took a variety of forms. The first rebels, the early feminists of the 1960s, accepted that biological factors divided women and men, and they identified women's anatomical and reproductive differences as the crucial problem. These differences meant that women had been trapped in limiting lifestyles and made dependent upon men. Nevertheless, the feminist writers rejected these consequences as inevitable. Their slogan "biology is destiny" became in effect a rally-ing cry. Women must refuse to allow their sexuality to be mapped out for them. It was their responsibility to stop biology from becoming destiny. As a result, these feminists put forward new ideas for limit-ing the effects of sexual differences, especially the force of women's reproductive role.

Two of these became widespread demands, held up on placards at every demonstration of American feminists. They wanted legal-ized abortion and twenty-four-hour nursery care. Abortion, in par-ticular, was regarded as a central plank of women's liberation. Those advocating it felt it would free women from having to continue with unwanted pregnancies and give them choice about what to do with their own bodies. No one else had the moral right to tell women what they should do. In America, the debate surrounding abortion affected the progress of the Equal Rights Amendment. The Amend-ment, introduced into Congress every year since 1923, was an attempt to outlaw discrimination against women by amending the Constitution. It had passed both the House of Representatives and the Senate in 1972, and by 1978 thirty-four state legislatures had ratified the amendment. Yet, because it was connected, implicitly, to abortion rights, it was strongly opposed by the New Right in the 1980s and has never received the necessary "three-quarters of states" ratification.

In Britain, the Abortion Reform Law was passed in 1968, but the campaigning continued. The requirements laid down by the law still fell far short of abortion on demand, and women were not free to make the decision entirely for themselves. Other people were involved in the approval for abortion process, and many restrictions remained in place. This remains the legal position today, and, with some caveats, rightly so. Abortion is a profoundly social and moral issue, not sim-ply a matter of individual choice of whether to allow a pregnancy to result in childbirth. The very least the law can do is offer some safe-guards, both for women and their children.

Safeguards were not uppermost in the minds of the early femi-nist writers. Some of their other suggestions went even further in the attempt to even out the biological imbalances between women and men. Some argued that legalized abortion had as its focus the "masculinization" of women in that the aim of the abortion-on-demand lobby was to enable women to make the sorts of decisions that were available only to those who did not have to carry babies, i.e., men. But we could argue that other, more radical, measures had as their focus the "feminization" of men, for the aim of the "biological manipulation" lobby was to move toward the effective eradication of difference.

The idea was to give men the opportunity to experience the limitations of women's biology and release women from being sole carriers of these burdens. In particular, proponents of these ideas suggested that men should be enabled to share the physical task of childbearing, which penalized so many women and restricted their freedom in the world of work. This could be done if a temporary substitute womb could be produced in the male body by surgically adapting the bladder.[2] This "womb" could then carry an embryo fathered by the man and transplanted from his female partner and serve as a temporary home until the embryo reached full term. The suggestion was made with enthusiasm and widely discussed (along with ideas for freeing women by transplanting the human embryo into the uterus of a large mammal). Yet it was not taken seriously by more than a handful of people and was more widely regarded as science fiction. It would take another twenty years before the eminent British science magazine, *New Scientist,* hailed the suggestion as a medical possibility.[3]

Along with the skepticism about the workability of these suggestions, something else was changing within the modernist mentality. There was a growing unease, among feminists themselves, about what they were surrendering with this kind of response to essentialism. All the earlier suggestions had addressed the apparent symptoms and had tried, in some way or another, to change the impact of biology. But the feminist writers had not delved beneath the symptoms to make sure they had their diagnosis right. In fact, they left the underlying assumptions of premodernity intact; biology stayed the focus of the issue. The greatest limitation of these early modern writers is that they did not challenge the implicit notion that the fundamental definition of woman was a biological one. They simply brought forward proposals to ameliorate its effects.

37

BIOLOGY IS NOT DESTINY

There had to be another way of rebelling against biological essentialism, and that way was, quite simply, to reject its claims. The next group of writers did just that. They argued that biology was "itself part of the ideology of gender inequality, rather than an independent authority which can offer neutral arbitration on the 'facts.'"[4] The new modernist writers, therefore, refused to buy into the old perspective and set to work mounting a critique of its assumptions. They worked from alternative presuppositions and with an alternative commitment. Biology did not provide any framework for understanding what was essential in human relationships. In fact, if anything was essential regarding male and female, it was a common humanity. And that common humanity highlighted some very important things, not least the need for mutual justice and equality.

The new perspective moved away from biological reductionism, and once old assumptions about the primacy of biology were discarded, all kinds of new possibilities were opened up. For example, instead of getting hung up on differences between women and men, people looked at their *similarities,* for men and women are really quite alike. They reflect one another in all kinds of characteristics such as capabilities, intellect, and stamina. Men organize, women organize; women teach, men teach; men heal the sick, women heal the sick. Women in the past had simply not been given the chance to develop their assets as fully and freely as they could. Once they did, however, and were given equality in law, education, and training, women would have access to roles usually occupied by men. Then the gender-segregated structure of society would begin to collapse.

THE JOURNEY FROM SEX TO GENDER

The new rebellion, therefore, finally departed fundamentally and decisively from premodernity. To do so, however, two key ideas had to be rejected. The first was the notion of the "natural," which had to be replaced very thoroughly with the "social." The argument here was clear: Human beings are socially constructed, not biologically created. Being a human person is not just about instincts or drives; that would be animal behavior. As humans we think and act. We are as much products of social change as of any biological evolution, so much so, in fact, that any differences can only be clearly understood when they are seen in their social location. For example, behind all ethnic, sexual, or class divergences are social, economic, and political factors. The real issues that matter about ethnic comparisons are not the differences in skin pigmentation but the differences in income, privilege, promotion, opportunity, customs, dress, religion, language, and so on. Similarly, comparisons between women and men must be made against a backdrop of attitudes, access, expectations, and control rather than focusing on their reproductive differences. As one writer observed, "If race, sex and class were not politically and economically significant categories, it is likely that no one would care very much about biological differences between members of these groups."[5] With this greater awareness of the social dimensions of the debate, modernity shifted away from the genetic, reproductive, and physiological differences of biology to the way society was structured and the roles that resulted. The key to change would be the way those factors were addressed.

The second idea modernists needed to reject was the oversimplified idea of "sex" in favor of the more complex notion of "gender," for sex—being male and female—was obviously not an adequate category for understanding the complexities of man-woman relationships. So much of what occurs in those relationships is not about sex but about gender—being masculine or feminine. And "masculine" and "feminine" are cultural concepts related to nurture, expectations, and social traditions. Germaine Greer explains: "Masculinity is to maleness as femininity is to femaleness. That is to say that maleness is the natural condition, the sex if you like, and masculinity is the cultural construct, the gender."[6] So being a man and a woman is as much about *learning* to be masculine and feminine as it is about living with one's differences in chromosomes. For example, people in different cultures learn different ways of being masculine and feminine, or men and women, according to the attitudes and expectations that are prevalent. The new diagnosis was clear: Most of the problems in social relationships were not caused by any biological differences between male and female; they were caused by what society *did* with those differences.

39

The modernists, therefore, challenged both the reductionism of the premodern mind and its espousal of biology as an explanatory framework. With the changing of the discourse, the old arguments about the biological differences between male and female were left behind, and a new appraisal of how the culture interprets and presents the differences between men and women took their place.

WHERE IS THE EVIDENCE?

The evidence for this new argument was easy to find. Sociologists took a look at the so-called sexual division of labor, for example, and found that the different roles occupied by the male and female workforce were not related predominantly to muscle or physical size but to social values and attitudes about men and women. This was evident even by the 1970s and became much more obvious once the silicon chip revolutionized the nature of work and made any biological differences virtually irrelevant.

It is significant that gender differentials remain in many areas of work, even in those areas in which work does not require hard physical labor and women and men have been equally trained for the same task. Even at the beginning of the third millennium, in most of the world's most advanced societies, men still overwhelmingly occupy the most well-paid, higher-status positions, and in some areas women have been engaged in a continual battle to be accepted at all. The premodern justification was that men and women are biologically suited for different types of work (and levels of pay!). But that argument cannot be sustained in an era that has left a biological-related work structure behind. In most of the professions and much of the business world today, division of labor has much more to do with how women and men are evaluated, who makes the decisions, and how hierarchies are designed.

There are complex issues involved in other areas of male-female relationships. Take, for example, the area of violence toward women. It had been long assumed under premodern notions that domestic violence, incest, and sexual assault were caused largely by instinctual, biological urges that men could not control. Indeed, sociobiology suggested that such action was an inevitable part of the way societies evolve. Yet, it is now much more widely recognized that much violence toward women is the result of the deliberate excercise of male power, aided by the unconscious collusion of a male-dominant society. To relate violence simply to uncontrollable primitive drives and instincts grossly misses the point. Indeed, some researchers argue that such violence is often very controlled. A medical practitioner called upon to treat many women subject to domestic violence documents how precise and measured such attacks can be. He points out that a domestic abuser will often assault his victim through suffocation but will relinquish hold at exactly the point before she is asphyxiated.[7] Similarly, evidence from studies on violence in fundamentalist households points to the alarming way in which some men use highly controlled violence as a way of "disciplining" their wives and bringing them into line.

It is interesting, in passing, to ask why so much violence in the home has traditionally gone unreported. This is also true in cases of rape, especially when the rapist is known to the victim. The reasons are not unrelated to the discussion. One predominant response from the victims is that they feel ashamed. (This is true, incidentally, whether the violence is suffered by either women or men.) They feel that the behavior of a violent spouse, partner, or colleague reflects negatively on their own value and worth, and on their "femininity" or "masculinity." It is a telling indication of the force of social attitudes. In a different context of violence, shame from the victim would not be the response. If a storekeeper, for example, were to endure a brutal assault during a burglary, he might feel angry and outraged or cautious and nervous in the future, but he is unlikely to feel ashamed. Values, which attach themselves to gendered behavior, are complex and are shaped both by current ideologies of men and women and also by power structures.

POWER AND PATRIARCHY

This concept of power is, therefore, one of the key sociopolitical hinges of the modernists. They argue that it lies at the heart of both economic relations and sexual ones (the "personal is also political"), and in this conjunction lies the ability to create patriarchy. Speaking bluntly, we have constructed cultures that have rewarded men for being men and penalized women for being women. Built into most of these societies are attitudes and practices that divide men and women into different groups with clearly distinctive roles, and then reinforce and elevate men's roles while belittling or even deriding women's roles. Reality itself has been viewed predominantly through the viewpoint of the male, and consequently, we have not questioned the idea that men should be the dominant sex and women the subservient. The problem is that cultures have fooled millions of people into thinking this is normal. Yet, nothing is simply normal or natural. What becomes accepted as "normal" in any given society is a social and political construct of those in power, the elites who are able to maintain the status quo.

We can see this point illustrated by returning to our story of the Second World War and its aftermath, for modernist writers offered a very different reading of our postwar gender history. For them, there was nothing normal about the different ways in which men and women functioned during this period. Instead, they insisted that "normality" was ideologically reconstructed in the 1950s to ensure that the key task of the day could be accomplished. Far from being natural and biological, the driving force was political motivation.[8]

This new reading of the story showed that even during the war, gender roles had not simply gone along "biological" lines. Although women had not been part of the fighting forces, they had contributed to the war economy in many capacities; certainly they took on jobs of domestic service, nursing, and ancillary and clerical services, but they were also in munitions, heavy industry, and manufacturing. Women had worked as shipbuilders, welders, furnace workers, engine drivers—in fact, all the jobs previously seen as only men's work. Even physical work was shown to be not simply about muscle power but about organization, cooperation, and team spirit.

What happened at the end of the war was also interesting. It was assumed in Britain and the rest of Europe that most women were only too glad to get away from the furnaces and back to the home. And this was true. Yet, in many areas, including parts of the United States, women strongly resisted the movement back to domesticity.

In the film *Rosie the Riveter,* a Brooklyn Jewish woman, one of many women who found themselves displaced after the men returned, explained how during the war, when she had been working as a first-grade welder in a munitions factory, she had one dream. She wanted, in peacetime, to make something beautiful and constructive out of the iron that she had welded to produce weapons of destruction. Most of all she wanted to make a magnificent, ornate wrought iron gate—something that would be her own contribution to peaceful elegance and grace. Yet, her dream was never realized because she, like the other women, was summarily dismissed. Working women were required to vacate their jobs for the returning men and go back to housework or domestic ancillary employment. From being productive and esteemed she was now involuntarily "unproductive," doing nonwork as far as official statistics and social status were concerned.

In writings and film, the postwar period was portrayed not as a time of the "normal" outworking of "natural" gender roles, but as a time when normality was reinvented to suit the ideology of the decision makers. No government could afford to have its returning servicemen face unemployment. There would soon be serious questions about the sacrifice of life if war veterans could not be honored by meaningful work. There was also the long-term possibility of civil unrest. So women had to go. Government propaganda films were part of the process. Archive film in the United States shows how women were manipulated to make them fall in line with official policy. Women who had been encouraged to leave their children in the crèche were now rebuked for being heartless mothers. Housewives who had been given survival recipes for food for immediate consumption were now given recipes that took four days to cook. Women who had previously worked unself-consciously alongside men were now depicted as unfeminine and competitive. By exposing this archive material and giving their own interpretation of what had happened, the feminists of the 1970s and beyond challenged every explanation that appealed simplistically to biology.

The Captive Wife?

During this time, the feminists also put family roles under the spotlight. The premodern notion had been that a woman's place in the family was based on sex differences. Being by nature more nurturing, it was natural that women and not men should be in charge of raising children. And being by nature more instinctual, they should be in the home where these traits could flourish. Even though they did not contribute to the hard economic production necessary for any society to survive, women's biology equipped them for the child-rearing and domestic work that provided a supportive substructure for the work process.

New research in the social sciences began to challenge all that. To start with, the premise was attacked as false. "Women weren't raising children because they were hard-wired to be more loving, but because they were shut out of higher education and discriminated against in the paid labour force."[9] When this changed and women were admitted equally to these areas, the likelihood was that the ideology of woman-as-homemaker would change. Similarly, the idea that women were "unproductive" in the home was revisited and rejected, for every society's economy depended on the "unpaid" services of women.

This new interest in gender was keenly reflected in studies on domesticity. Areas once deemed too insignificant for study now became noteworthy. Ann Oakley wrote a substantial study titled *Sociology of Housework,* following it with a best-selling paperback, *Woman's Work: The Housewife, Past and Present.*[10] She documented widespread dissatisfaction with the monotony, fragmentation, and relentlessness of women whose lives were spent predominantly in keeping house.[11] Their biology did not fit them for that! Hannah Gavron's book, *The Captive Wife,*[12] looked at women's perceptions of intimate relationships within the home, and again the picture was not one of unparalleled bliss. The younger women in her sample compared their mothers' expectations with their own, and already a new picture emerged of what was expected in marriage: not a reinforcement of old roles, but a development of new intimacy. Women wanted husbands who would cherish them and treat them as equals and companions. (The fact that in Britain three-quarters of all divorces are now initiated by women suggests that, sadly, this message may not yet have gotten through.)

The underlying assumptions of these writers of modernity were thus at odds with their premodern antecedents. With the focus now on gender, not sex, there was a different response to inequality. Whereas the former had believed that inequality was a justifiable and predictable outworking of biological difference, the latter believed it was due to the exercise of power relationships and was never justifiable. The new analysis could not remain merely analytical. Once the diagnosis was given, it inevitably had to lead to the kind of action that would bring about more equal relationships, which required that men willingly give up power and be ready for change.

EQUALITY, SIMILARITY, AND DIFFERENCE

If the underlying assumption of the premoderns was biological "difference," the focus of modernist equality feminism was "similarity." ("It is virtually impossible to separate the idea of equality from the idea of similarity."[13]) It now seemed that the deep similarity between women and men had been masked by the constructions of a gender identity that was oppositional. "Far from being an expression of natural differences exclusive gender identity is the suppression of natural similarities."[14] Unequal treatment, unequal access to power, unequal participation in decision making all hide those similarities, and therefore, the task of feminism became to challenge and change these structures. Once there was a commitment to change, any differences in biology would no longer be relevant to how the lives of men and women were lived out in society.

But there were different groups of modernist feminists, and not all of them were in agreement with this analysis, however. Some stressed the importance of separation for women and men. These separatist feminists were not interested in working alongside men in an attempt to bridge the gap caused by a patriarchal society, for as far as they were concerned, men themselves constituted the problem. The important issue for them was straightforward: to effect a radical improvement in the lives of women. But when women had not only been marginalized but actually defined by assumptions of patriarchy, the first task was to challenge those definitions and allow women to speak for themselves. In order for women to develop their own voice, therefore, they needed space from men, and they needed space in every area in which they had previously been subordinated by men. Separatist feminism criticized equality feminism as optimistic and naive—optimistic in its

45

view of social change and naive in its assumptions about the effectiveness of legislation. They believed a search for equality kept men constantly as the reference point, but an assertion of difference offered more openness.

However, most people recognized that whether they argued for equality or difference, such arguments in no way guaranteed liberation for women. In a society in which those who have the privileges do not want to lose them, arguments can always be "neutralized" by clever footwork. Germaine Greer points out:

> A male soldier who wants the right to wear long hair pleads equality; a male tennis player who wants to go on being paid twice as much as his mixed doubles partner will plead difference. A man who wants paternity leave will plead equality, a member of the Marylebone Cricket Club who wants to exclude women will plead difference.[15]

Real freedom depends more on the structures and attitudes that lie underneath the appeal either to similarity or difference. And many of those are not open to logic.

A New Essentialism

Although the thrust of modernism was anti-essentialist, it was clear that the modernists did not dispense with essentialism altogether. They had their own explanatory frameworks, their own "metanarratives." They replaced the metanarratives of the premoderns—biology, natural order, normality—with new ones that more clearly fitted their own assumptions, and the focus differed depending on whether they were liberal moderns, socialist moderns, or radical moderns.[16] They all agreed on the identification of the problem: Biology and nature had been offered as a justification for inequality and oppression. They disagreed as to how they identified its source.

Liberal moderns (predominantly equality feminists) argued that it was a result of poor education, representation, and legislation, and thus set about reforming the education and legal systems to help more women gain positions of authority, decision making, and leadership.

46

The socialist moderns said it was a result of a deeper problem: economic injustice and the class system. They saw a strong parallel between production and reproduction and argued that women were an underclass behind men. Therefore, they threw their weight behind a critique of capitalism and a political program for the future.

The radicals (usually separatist feminists) rejected both these ways out, deriding both the legislative and socialist utopias. In their view, socialist men were just as sexist as capitalist men. In capitalism, "man exploits man." In socialism, it is the other way round! In fact, neither cares about the oppression of women. Therefore, a new diagnosis of the problem was born, focusing not on representation, legislation, or economic inequality, but on *men*. The radicalism was typified in the American organization SCUM (the Society for Cutting Up Men). "Patriarchy" became the key concept to describe the relations between men and women. And what, in their view, did patriarchy use to justify male dominance? Biology and sexuality. Ultimately, sexuality was political and had been interpreted by a deeply sexist system.

The allegation was a simple one. Whether in marriage and family relationships, in incest, rape, or sexual violence, women's sexuality was seen as belonging to men. Heterosexuality itself was not about equal sexual relations. It was about "men first." For the radical moderns, men had captured "normality," interpreted it in ways that suited them, and used it against women. This radical reading of feminism, especially with regard to sexuality, was to set the scene for a new series of debates. It would also provoke some vehement reactions from those who saw it as an overstatement of the difference between male and female behavior.[17]

47

THE ASSESSMENT FROM WITHIN FEMINISM

Although modernist feminism really belongs to the 1960s and 1970s, a new generation of young feminists was still writing from within the modernist metanarrative at the end of the twentieth century. Some of the arguments rehearsed in Natasha Walter's book *The New Feminism*, for example, sound surprisingly like the old liberal feminism of the thirty years prior.[18] In *On the Move,* published in 1999, a group of young women writers examine the same concerns that affected their "modernist" mothers and grandmothers, with very similar arguments and conclusions. Katherine Viner and Aminatta Forna are just two who believe women have been taken in by the lure of the pay packet and the sense of equality in the workplace. They look at the way top women executives are being persuaded to pose in girlie positions for men's magazines and challenge the notion that this is about liberation. In fact, they argue that at the end of the century the personal is more political than ever, "more political than when gender roles were more stratified because there is more up for grabs." Even if it had been achieved, equality at work would not be enough, for women's *sexuality* is still defined by a patriarchal society. Having the right to equal pay means little if women do not also have "the right for their body size to be unimportant, or . . . the right to an equal sexual relationship."[19]

This point is echoed by Germaine Greer, who was one of the pioneers of feminism in its modern phase. At the turn of the new millennium, she made an assessment of the gains achieved by women in the last thirty years. In her book *The Whole Woman,* Greer laments that in many areas of life, the situation is worse for women than it was when she wrote *The Female Eunuch.* She questions whether even the changes in the law actually delivered for women the freedom that they were intended to, for when the power of patriarchy itself does not diminish, every piece of legislation can eventually become another way of producing oppression for women. In a poignant passage she wonders what ultimately women won even with the reform of the abortion law:

> What women "won" was the "right" to undergo invasive procedures in order to terminate unwanted pregnancies, unwanted not just by them but by their parents, their sexual partners, the governments who would not support mothers, the employers who would not employ mothers, the landlords who would not accept tenants with children, the schools that would not accept students with children. What abortion did was to make illiberal governments seem feminist.[20]

Yet, apart from these latest books, the debate has been taking a new direction. Today's climate is complex because much of the feminism that came out of the modernist ethos is itself under attack. It is dismissed as irrelevant by the "new woman" because women have "now got what they want," and simultaneously rejected by postmodern writers because they believe it is impossible to make universal statements about what "women" want.

Consequently, a new genre has been slowly shaping the questions about sex and gender, a genre that does not share the concepts and outlook of the modern writers. A different, *postmodern* response had already bitten deeply into the feminism of the 1980s and challenged its own assumptions. And it was not simply some despondency with the *results* of the feminism of modernity that triggered off the postmodern position. It was a shift of philosophical underpinnings.

The question whether our sexuality is constructed or created had been, up to this point, a debate between premodernity and modern feminism. Premodernity saw all differences rooted in sexuality. Modernity based its arguments on a distinction between sex (created) and gender (constructed). But now the debate was to take on a new emphasis. Postmodernity rejected the precedence given to biology and sexuality by the premoderns. But it also began to reject the differentiation between sex and gender of the moderns. Instead, it argued that all identity, indeed all sexuality, was itself constructed. A comment made twenty years earlier had forecast this. Ruth Hubbard said in 1981, "In our critique of biology, one thing becomes clear: not only must we not believe that biology is our destiny: we must re-examine whether it is even our biology."[21]

A paradox lay at the heart of feminism. Elaine Graham identified it succinctly: "In asserting equality with men, feminists refer to shared experience of oppression, which is identified as unique and distinctive to women alone."[22] In other words, if women's experience of oppression is peculiar to women, how can this undergird their equality with men? Inevitably, the new thinkers were ready to contest the entire concept of equality and replace it with the notion of women's uniqueness. The debate was once again about difference—although a different difference from that of premodernity! Gone now was the essentialism of biology, but gone also was what the new writers saw as the essentialism of modernity: the location of gender identity in patterns of learning, expectations, and power structures. Instead, for the postmoderns there are no essentials, no metanarratives, no overriding explanatory frameworks.

The interpretations of a very different group of writers was therefore to take the debate into another new phase and shake the very contours of what had been accepted before. Any sense of the givenness or createdness of the nature of women and men was to bow before the insistence that everything is constructed. Not only biology but even the patriarchal oppression of women was to be understood as itself a social construct that relies on some "location in a social discourse." The big question was whether postmodern feminism could ever produce a program for change.

4

THE POSTMODERN EXPERIENCE

E ven though some writers at the end of the twentieth century had revived a modernist position, the arguments of modernity had increasingly receded over the last decade of the century. In 1992, French postmodern writer Luce Irigaray insisted that we were "at a different stage of History."[1] In 1994, Jean Joseph Goux suggested that the modernist phase was coming to a close. Its concerns had been superseded, its battles were not now relevant. For Goux, the cultural changes had finally seen off the old ways of thinking. In particular the obsession with defeating the biological essentialists had run its course. "One might go so far as to say: essentialism is no longer a danger for it is no longer even thinkable. . . . In a world dominated by the market and the media . . . and the inconvertibility of circulating values, something completely different is at stake."[2]

For postmodern people, that "something different" is the ability to live with the fluidity of shifting images and styles. It is the capacity to negotiate our own identity without needing someone else to define for us who we are, for in a market-media reality we recognize there are a multiplicity of options from which to shape our own style and choose our own values. We do not need to battle against outmoded world-views or absolutist explanations to try to establish an "Archimedean" point because there can be no such vantage point outside the constructs that fashion who we are and from which we can survey reality. We need simply to learn to live at ease within a pluralism of meanings and choices.

For most social commentators, postmodernity marks the end of any single, unifying worldview that attempts to offer universally valid explanations. It makes little difference to the postmodern mind whether those explanations were based on concepts of biology or power structures. They were still making an appeal to some grand narrative, some fundamental set of values or explanatory framework that would hold good for all times. Such an endeavor is now seen as fundamentally mistaken. As David Harvey points out, postmodernity represents a "total acceptance of the ephemeral fragmentation and discontinuity of life."[3] Postmodern concerns are with surface rather than depth, with representations rather than the search for ultimate truth. For what is truth? Only what Friedrich Nietzsche suggested: "a mobile army of metaphors, metonyms and anthropomorphisms."[4]

Therefore, we do not need to draw any demarcation between representation and reality, for images are as "real" as anything that purports to lie behind them. Nor do we need to study the past to try to find "truth" there, for the past is significant only in its ability to be experienced in the present. In postmodern culture, present experience is the only reality we know, and we can know it without trying to grasp any extra dimension of "meaning" outside the process of experience. Language, image, and experience come together, playfully and creatively, their meaning constructed or decided according to cultural convention. We are part of the constructive process, presenting what we will as pastiche, metaphor, or symbol. We choose options and style as we wish.

A postmodern critique addresses both modernists and premodernists, for neither has escaped intransigence. Its own commitment is to deconstruction, the questioning and dismantling of all that we previously thought of as real. There are no boundaries to what can be deconstructed. We can include the past, the present, categorical explanations, concepts, language, meaning, sexuality, biology, sociology, and theology. In the process of deconstruction, we discover that what were once thought of as "absolutes" are only particulars, and even these particulars can be seen through myriad different perspectives depending on the location of the perceiver. Lars Johansson sums up the procedure and its effects:

> The postmodern deconstructs the metanarrative of the Western tradition, leaving us with a plurality of narratives and values. One of the metanarratives that has been disclosed is reason. Central to the critique of reason is language. All thinking begins and ends in language. Philosophy is seen as rhetoric in disguise. There is no independent vantage point outside language.[5]

The result is a position that locates us always within some discourse, whose parameters are structured by the words and concepts that give it meaning. There is no shared meta-language reflecting a reality that exists outside particular discourses. What is more, the words we use, the *signifiers,* do not signify that something actually exists "outside" the words, for "signification only ever refers back to itself, that is to say to another signification. Each time we are obliged in the analysis of language to look for the signification of a word, the only correct method is to enumerate all of its uses."[6] It is simply the use of language that decides its meaning, not any correspondence to some reality that exists outside.

This view has had repercussions in many disciplines, not simply in cultural or linguistic studies. It has been one of the prevailing influences in contemporary theology, for example in the earlier views of Don Cupitt, in the ideas of the "Sea of Faith." It has been expressed as an "outsidelessness" position, the view "that there is nothing beyond or outside human beings, neither Love, nor divinity, nor some other notion like 'Ultimate Reality' that gives life and meaning and purpose."[7] Language is "a disastrous mental illusion" from which there is no escape.

If language constructs reality, we can bring anything into being. Our words create politics, sexuality, history, God. In that sense, the

53

word is more powerful than it has ever been. But it has an uncertain and ambiguous power—not the power of "rendering past lives more coherent and less conflictful than they were" but the power to "recognize the instability of all categories, the contested terrain of all historical sites, the dangers in all political projects."[8] For what is left of history other than competing interpretations of the present? What is sexuality other than ideas in the mind? And who is God, other than a concept shaped by those who wish to give a name to an experience?

Deconstructing Modernist Feminism

In this climate, the language of modernity is seen to have had deep internal contradictions, especially within the discourse of equality feminism. As Elaine Graham explains:

> Deconstructionist philosophies and strategies claim that "equality" and "difference" are not absolutes, but are themselves constructs. They emerge from human discourse and exist within a context of power relations and material practice. To attempt to impose absolute and unchanging meaning on gender relations is to assert an abstraction which returns us to metaphysics.[9]

Within modernity, language about sex and gender was still being used as though there was some fixed meaning to these terms, something that existed objectively. The modernists believed they had highlighted the part that social construction plays in our identity. They thought they had eliminated essentialism by changing the categories from sex to gender. Some of them conceded that our sexuality might in some sense be biologically "given," but they did not see that as important, for even if sexual differences do exist objectively, they are of limited significance and always subsumed under the dynamic of gender. Yet, these writers apparently failed to recognize that the attempt to avoid biological determinism by emphasizing a sex-gender distinction simply opened up a different form of absolutism. Instead of biology, the new constituents of gender identity were cultural roles, patterns of learning, and socially imposed norms. There was always some reference to an objective reality "out there," some assumption of an explanatory framework that gave our signifiers meaning. This was because, however far it had moved from the notion of creation to construction, modernity was still working with the notion of a "core identity," both in ourselves and our relationships.

Postmodern critics saw other problems too. Modernity had attempted to critique and replace the system of male domination with a radical egalitarianism. Now, it was inevitable that this attempt would ultimately fail, for equality feminism never escaped the assumptions of the system it tried to undermine. As far as Goux is concerned, it did not see that its own language and concepts absorbed the very male domination it was trying to counter, for "without intending it, egalitarian claims are complicit with the deep logic of this domination."[10] Equality feminism rested too heavily on the notion of similarity and underplayed the significance of sex in favor of that of gender. It failed to recognize that "both 'sex' and 'gender' are woven of multiple, asymmetrical strands of difference, charged with multifaceted, dramatic narratives of domination and struggle."[11] Indeed, within the modernist critique, it would seem that sex disappeared altogether as a significant category. Everything was swallowed up by gender. The question is, however, by which gender? Luce Irigaray and others are quite clear: the male gender. Equality is predicated on women's parity *with men,* and so the norm remains male.

The assumption had been that to lift gender roles out of power relationships would bring both equality and gender neutrality. Yet, for those who take a postmodern stance, it could never do this. An egalitarianism that rests on the abandonment of difference is the most subtle way yet of making women invisible, for tradition, language, and concepts have for too long all been formed within a male dominant framework. Espousing "equality" while everything else stays the same is to give the appearance of empowering women while denying the reality of it. It is in fact to capitulate to the deeper structures of patriarchy in the name of reform. Egalitarianism in effect means the disappearance of women. They are admitted into the structures but only as token or lesser men. According to Irigaray, for a woman to abandon her own sexual identity "represents the greatest possible submission to masculine culture."[12]

55

Women simply become absorbed within the male gender, into what Luce Irigaray calls the "masculine-neutral."

Where does that leave women's authenticity? Trapped in something "suicidal," "the worst expression of the extravagance of masculine intellectualism."[13] The argument is that women's identity can never be fully realized under a gender analysis, any more than it can be realized under biological essentialism. Gender identity "is ultimately a symptom of parasitic invasion, the expression within me of forces originating from the outside."[14] What we must do is find who we are from *within*. It is only in the real stuff of women's sexuate experience that we encounter our identity and must reclaim our sexuality for ourselves. Each woman has to discover her own subjectivity, stripped away from all the years of patriarchal interpretation, and she must do it as herself, in her own particularity, not as some inaccessible universal "woman." In Irigaray's words: "Beneath all those/her appearances, beneath all those/her borrowed finery, that female other still sub-sits."[15] Sex, therefore, becomes deconstructable and reconstructable into experiences that women can choose to appropriate for themselves.

CREATED OR CONSTRUCTED?

We thus arrive at the farthest point from the notion that our sexuality and human identity have some kind of fixed, irreducible center, and it is precisely here that the postmodern writers return to the concept of difference. They are no longer afraid of the essentialism, the notions of fixed sexual identity that had kept women locked into submission, for as Goux believes, it is now out of view. They recognize the suspicion and misunderstandings that might greet this move back to a concept that has a checkered history, "and the guarantees it will need to offer if it is not simply to be confused with a return to pre-modern prejudices."[16] But this sexual difference is no longer predicated on anything that is "natural" or fixed or defined within a masculine-shaped reality. Difference is now self-defined and fluid. As Toril Moi points out, "Differences always take us elsewhere, we might say, involve us in an ever proliferating network of displacement and deferral of meaning."[17]

At one level, therefore, postmodernity offers a far more intense critique of gender than anything that has come before because it challenges the very linguistic processes we use as being imbued with masculine-constructed meaning. What the modernist writers had offered as processes of differentiating, separating, analyzing are now seen themselves as gender-loaded, for all of these are activities shaped within a discourse dominated by the masculine. Even the terms of the debate to which this book is committed are questionable, for I have been talking as though "constructed" and "created" refer to two polar opposites, two competing explanations, which we decide on by reference to arguments that match the realities and facts "out there." But from a postmodern perspective, in approaching the issue this way I have merely absorbed and reflected the thought processes that have predominated in a male-shaped discourse. There are no polarities other than what *we* make polar, no opposites other than what *we* decide to create. What is more, there is no "out there," for this is itself only a linguistic construct.

The only viable way forward in opening up an understanding of identity and sexuality is through experience. For Luce Irigaray and Julia Kristeva this means through women's experience. For an increasing number of male writers, it means through men's experience. But this process cannot be regarded as a new kind of essentialism, for just as women and men are different, so men and men are different, and women and women are different. We have to reject some uniform notion of human experience or even of sexual-gendered experience and see that "difference itself is multiple, conditioned by the factors of class, region, sexuality and culture."[18] With a focus on narrative rather than analysis, we listen to and absorb the experiences of all women: black and white, rich and poor, powerful and marginalized, immigrant and indigenous, straight and gay, old and young. It is not the job of the theorist to choose between them or to pass judgment on them. We simply hear their stories.

So just as there can be no one gender analysis of the oppression of women, so there is no one sexual analysis of the identity of women. Our sexuality, like all the rest of life, is in a constant process of construction. The problem comes in moving from critique to action, from deconstruction to a new ethical imperative. Nothing is being offered as the way forward. Nothing is held up for us to appropriate. Neither natural sexuality nor gender equality shapes any new political engagement. What we have instead is "the quest for a social and cultural sexuation whose eventual outcome one cannot, by definition, foresee, any more than one can invent overnight the characteristic forms and style of a civilisation."[19]

SO, WHO AM I?

All of this has predictable consequences. First, we have to make our own way, decide for ourselves what it is to be a woman or a man. Philip and Miriam Sampson make the obvious point:

> Once our "natural sexuality" ceases to define a "real woman" (or man) it is obvious that there is no "natural" way of being a "man" at all for there are a wide variety of cultural styles of masculinity to choose from or to combine: from Rambo to Julian Clary, from the "new laddism" to the "new man," from straight to gay. Gender identity is constructed, not inherited, "and is composed of an amalgam, of images which already exist in the culture around us."[20]

But this puts enormous emphasis on the process of choosing an identity, especially when there are no constraints on that choice. How do we choose when there are no underlying ethical reasons why some choices are good and others are bad? Having the freedom and space to choose from a multiplicity of identities is not much gain if it does not matter what I choose. There can be no coherent critique of those who choose to reinforce an old patriarchal lifestyle, if this, after all, is their preference. The muddy waters of relativism are never far from a postmodern critique, and relativism can never give us a framework for strategies for change.

But it is not only that difference is "unable to reflect the complexity of lived experience at the same time as sketching a theoretical reconfiguration."[21] Nor is it only that choice becomes thereby emptied as a concept. With postmodern fragmentation comes the erasure of the category of self. We move from being who and what we are as the result of some personal essence to how we are constructed in various social groups. Kenneth Gergen writes, "[T]he initial stages of this consciousness result in a sense of the self as a social con artist, manipulating images to achieve ends." But who or what is it that is being constructed, for even to talk of the construction of self implies something I can identify as personal identity. "As the category of 'real self' continues to recede from view, however, one acquires a pastiche-like personality."[22]

The other unanswered question is whether postmodernity can ever deliver a version of difference that avoids the essentialist pitfalls derided by its premodern and modern predecessors. How can we locate or even talk about women's difference unless we describe it in terms that are identifiable? And once we have identified it, whether in terms of the "jouissance" of some pre-oedipal stage or the existence of some "feminine fluidity"—inner space, movement, flux, "becoming"—why is this not also a kind of essentialism?[23] The answer is not clear, except insofar as the deconstructionists assert that they are creating only limited analogies, not developing another theory of being.

Irigaray believes that in discovering and constructing their own sexuality, women are not discovering anything that exists independently in some kind of female core, uncontaminated by patriarchal values. Authentic sexuality is rather the development of "sites of resistance" to such values. Similarly, in offering us a concept of "polymorphous sensuality," Irigaray insists she is not offering this as "a 'true' or accurate description of women. Its function is not referential, but combative. . . . It does not designate a female essence or anatomy but subverts the dominant male conceptions of women's essence."[24] But this is dangerously close to semantic and rhetorical manipulation. This explanation seems to say little more than that a description of what constitutes female difference is not really a description. It is simply a denial of a patriarchal construction and as such leaves everything open. It is at this cost that postmodernity retains both plurality and fragmentation and nudges women into designing their own subjectivity.

With the postmodern response, our journey thus arrives at a place of ambiguity and uncertainty. At best, we might see this response as irony, as playing, ironically, with old patriarchal concepts of sexuality and re-presenting them to shape and design an alternative perspective. More realistically, we might feel we are trapped within a self-referenc-

59

ing system, for when words are used without any suggestion that any of the models to which they refer could ever actually exist, then the meaning of language becomes fraught with complications. What is more, how do we know when to stop deconstructing and accept the position we have now arrived at? Nothing within the *process* of deconstruction can help us with that. Instead, we are caught up in an infinite regress, where each deconstruction can be further deconstructed, and no single text can ever make a definitive statement, including the text I am writing here.[25] In this way we cannot say whether human sexual identity is constructed and not created, for each of these terms is itself a linguistic construction, signifying nothing beyond. We cannot even say what constitutes gender identity, for ultimately, there is no identity to be had, only a series of experiences.

The question, then, is, Where do we go from here? And the answer is not clear. But as we shall see later, the lack of clarity has not prevented a postmodern perspective from finding its way into many areas of feminist thinking, including feminist theology. There, as everywhere, it throws up challenges for others, which, from its own perspective, it cannot meet itself.

Postmodernity has also penetrated popular culture, and questions of identity, meaning, and personhood are raised relentlessly in films and novels. In recent years, issues of what it means to be male and female have been worked through in films such as *Fight Club, American Beauty, Magnolia, American Psycho,* and scores of others. Although the presentation of these issues in novels, music, and film is very different from their presentation in the Franco-feminists, the underlying deconstruction, ambiguity, and relativism remain evident.

Not all aspects of popular culture reflect a postmodern position, however, even on the issues of sex and gender. The next chapter looks at contemporary authors who reflect something quite different.

GENDER AND "DIFFERENCE" IN POPULAR WRITINGS

nlike the modernist feminism of the 1960s, the writings of the postmodern theorists have not translated readily from academia to a good fireside read. Admittedly, the academic sophistication of Luce Irigaray, Jean Joseph Goux, or Rosi Braidotti was not evident in the 1960s popular blockbusters such as Betty Friedan's *The Second Sex* or Germaine Greer's *Female Eunuch*. Yet, these were important books that both reflected and influenced the scholarship current at the time. The uncompromising critique and polemic analysis of the social science writings were also present in the popular best-sellers. Readers did not flinch from the call to dismantle power structures; rather, they took the volumes cheerfully to bed with them. What was the attraction of these books? They were accessible to anyone interested in society or gender. Not everyone may have agreed with what they read, but they could certainly understand it. By contrast, postmodern feminist theorists seem quite out of reach for most of the contemporary reading public. They do not make for pleasant after-dinner relaxation or travel easily as comfortable holiday reading. In fact, they seem to frighten off anyone who does not enjoy probing philosophical concepts or a complex francophone style of writing.

Paradoxically, many feminists allege that postmodern feminist theorists are out of touch with the women's movement. In fact, from the early days of Irigaray's writings (she had previously been regarded as a "lesbian separatist"), those from the women's movement were quick to accuse her of misrepresenting them. They disliked the implication that postmodernity had "seen through" their own "limitations." They rebuffed the accusation that their own arguments had been narrow, focusing on a single cause of oppression. This was not the case, they insisted, for "the explosion of writing, the multiplication of references were used in quite the opposite way, to suggest the diversity of outside influences and states of freedom conquered or rediscovered. Jubilation in all directions over new ways of life!" This breadth for them had now disappeared, as had the radical vision: "Luce Irigaray, by contrast, brings the most reactionary possible feelings into her work. . . . How could this changeless body be the source of a new destiny?"[1]

It is not only the self-congratulation of the postmodern writers that has got up their critics' noses. It is also their alleged obscurantism and self-indulgence. What is the point of lengthy analyses of women's "subjective inner space" when women's "public external space" is still vulnerable to violence, rape, and attack? Why waste precious time with erudite articles on "sites of jouissance" when so many women are still struggling with sites of poverty, single parenthood, or inadequate health resources? The irritation is evident. It is as if these new theorists never intended for their writings to be read by "ordinary" readers with ordinary concerns. They seem instead to have written either simply for themselves or for a few other elitist scholars.

Since the key contemporary theorists are inaccessible to a mass readership, what has filled the gap between the scholars and the populace? Certainly, contemporary best-sellers on male-female issues exist. And they certainly have addressed current key problems. But the books that have been sending their authors laughing to the bank since the mid-1990s are very unlike the tirades against power structures or the politics of gender written in the 1960s and 1970s.[2] These books have been replaced on the bargain shelves of America's bookshops predominantly by books of popular gender psychology. Many are light-hearted, some are polemic, some are tedious. Significantly, however, almost all of them focus on the idea of "difference." They reflect the newly revived interest in difference without the academic focus or background.

The very starting point for most of these authors is that women and men are different, and, for the most part, their aim is to identify the points of difference and offer advice on how to deal with them. Unlike the popular writers of the 1960s, however, most of the currently popular authors manage with barely a reference to the theoretical debates. Few seem concerned enough to look at the philosophical underpinnings of "difference" or to try to distinguish one theoretical viewpoint from another. They also seem virtually unaware of the discussions surrounding essentialism. Inevitably, this deficiency can have great drawbacks. Although some of these books are written by people who are aware of the complexity of gender ideas, many are not, and the debate between nature and culture becomes confused and bowdlerized. Some writers are also stuck in belligerently premodern essentialist assumptions without being remotely critical of their own position.

POPULAR PUBLICATIONS—A CONFUSED DEBATE

We can see such limitations in *Why Men Don't Iron,* an archetypal book from a premodern perspective that claims in its subtitle to be *The Real Science of Gender Studies.* It is peppered with appeals to biology and suggests that all gender differences are sex differences laid down in nature. Gender cultural terms *(masculinity)* are used interchangeably with sex biological terms *(maleness)* with predictable results. The author argues that if we ran society along "natural" lines, men (and thereby women) would be much happier. But men are apparently now under attack from a current political ideology that claims *they* need to change and that does not realize nature cannot be changed. So who is to blame for this new thinking?

Apparently, the chief culprit is postmodernity. The authors manage to lay much of the blame at the feet of postmodernists while show-

ing an embarrassing lack of understanding of the postmodern position. At times they even assume the postmoderns are trying to avoid
difference. ("The postmodernists want men to change, to become
indeed, more like women."[3]) At the same time, the authors confidently
maintain that their own assertions about differences are backed up by
something they call "science." ("Science has upset the egalitarian apple-
cart by conclusively showing that the sexes are distinct in how they
act and think."[4]) Yet, in spite of their fascination for quasi-scientific
jargon, their "science" sounds alarmingly like tired stereotypes used
for years to justify old gender roles. A few examples from *Why Men
Don't Iron* will make the point:

> A man enjoys a neurological high when he is faced by competition.
> . . . A woman is not equipped by biology to receive this neurological
> reward. Indeed, if anything, her reaction to competition will be anx-
> iety. (p. 192)

> His lower serotonin level also makes it difficult for him to persevere
> with a boring chore, because his reward circuitry is not switched on
> by this sort of tedious activity. (p. 255)

> The fact that men have lower monoamine oxidase levels than women
> means that they will be much better adapted to the pressures of high-
> risk jobs, whether that job is trading derivatives or landing high-per-
> formance fighters on to aircraft carriers. . . . It will be a very rare woman
> who possesses the low serotonin needed for her brain not to engage
> her caution-inducing frontal cortex as she hurtles in towards the deck.
> (p. 159)

> Men have a lower sensitivity to detail, which means he simply does
> not notice the dust as she does. . . . The stale socks and sweaty shirt
> don't bother him because they are among the pheromone-related smells
> that women are acutely aware of, but men do not detect. (p. 252)

> Some high t[estosterone] level males do marry, but they are 43% more
> likely to be divorced and 38% more likely to engage in extramarital
> sex. . . . The conclusion seems obvious. You can have a man, but you
> cannot have a man who feels, touches, cares and empathises like a
> woman, not if you want him to stay a man. (p. 265)

Books such as this make us realize two things. First, quoting science or statistics is utterly unhelpful without the careful research and safeguards necessary for their interpretation. There is much jargon here but little reliable content. Second, Jean Joseph Goux was wrong: Essentialism is not dead. Scholars might have given it a decent burial, but non-scholars are still capable of digging it up, dressing it in the newest fashion, and parading it down the catwalk.

What is interesting is that in attacking the idea of gender neutrality as a myth, these authors are oblivious to the fact that postmodern scholars, such as Goux, got there before them. Their reasons for the attack are, however, fundamentally different. Postmodernity argues that the "gender-neutral" hides a masculine bias by which "equal" women are still subsumed under categories that reflect male values. The new essentialists suggest that the "gender-neutral" hides a feminine bias by which women make unreasonable demands on men, thereby emasculating them.[5] And while the solution for these new premoderns is also to abandon the search for equality, it is not so that women can know the liberation of self-assigned difference. It is rather to recreate a society that is excited about competition, reinforces premodern gender demarcations, and allows men to be "real" men.

Most other popular authors, while also starting from the idea that men and women are different, manage to avoid the worst excesses illustrated here. Whereas *Why Men Don't Iron* is lamentable in its generalization and biological reductionism, John Gray's book *Men Are from Mars, Women Are from Venus*[6] is less judgmental and somewhat more friendly. It offers itself as a "practical guide for improving communication and getting what you want in your relationships." It still has definite essentialist overtones ("men are like this . . . women are like this . . .") and is written from a less than self-critical male perspective, yet the aim is less to justify stereotypes than to enable people to relate better to one another. To that end, it encourages women and men to identify their own needs and recognize those of the other. It is assumed of course that all men have generalized psychological needs, attitudes, and understandings, which women are not likely to recognize. And, once again, these needs are natural, evolved, or created, not constructed.

65

> Men are like rubber bands. When they pull away, they can stretch only
> so far before they come springing back. . . . Most women are surprised
> to realize that even when a man loves a woman, periodically he needs
> to pull away before he can get closer. Men instinctively feel this urge
> to pull away. It is not a decision or choice. It just happens. It is nei-
> ther his fault nor her fault. It is a natural cycle. (p. 92)

But Gray does not relate this "nature" to levels of serotonin,
monoamine oxidase, or needs for neurological highs. He suggests,
instead, that men and women come from different places. They live
metaphorically on different planets, Venus and Mars. They are formed
by different cultures and need to learn one another's languages and
thought patterns. The planetary differences between them extend to
every aspect of male-female relationships, including the way they handle emotions. Again, some examples will make the point.

> When a Venusian is upset she not only uses generalities and so forth,
> but also is asking for a particular kind of support. She doesn't directly
> ask for that support because on Venus everyone knew that dramatic
> language implied a particular request. (p. 62)

> It's easy for a woman to give what she needs and forget that her favorite
> Martian may need something else. Likewise, men tend to focus on
> their needs, losing track of the fact that the kind of love they need is
> not always appropriate for or supportive of their favorite Venusian.
> (p. 134)

> Martians give when they are asked. Martians pride themselves in being
> self-sufficient. They don't ask for help unless they really need it. On
> Mars, it is rude to offer help unless you are first asked. Quite the oppo-
> site, Venusians don't wait to offer their support. When they love some-
> one, they give in any way they can. (p. 193)

Although Gray gets too carried away with his metaphor, and his
book becomes repetitive and tiresome, its aim is benign: to release
women and men from the misunderstandings and wrong expectations
they have about each other. Men need to understand that women do
not read their responses in the way that men would; women need to

know that men do not hear what is being implied in the way women would. In that sense, the book takes the theme of difference, absorbs both a natural and a cultural perspective, and then plays it through in popular psychology, wrapping it up in counseling advice. Because it claims to be evenhanded in its approach and to give insights with which people can easily identify, it has become one of the most widely read texts on gender of the 1990s. Yet, it rests on essentialist assumptions that are never examined.

His later book, *Mars and Venus in the Bedroom,* is sadly far less evenhanded. It regurgitates a large number of stereotypes passed down in America through early Hollywood films and works through a haggard, old agenda, especially about sexual relations. For example, Gray warns women of the danger of giving out "rejecting messages" to their partners. Instead of refusing sexual intercourse when she doesn't feel like it, a woman should simply encourage a few "guilt-free quickies" or offer to give him "a hand job," otherwise the man "may begin desiring other women who have not yet rejected him, or he may just lose interest." Women, however, should be careful about initiating sex themselves, and especially too directly, as this puts undue pressure on men to perform, and they feel controlled. A woman should rather drop indirect hints that she is in a "hot, lusty and intense" mood by wearing "black lace or garters," or that she wants "sensitive, gentle and loving sex" by putting on her nightie of white silky satin. A short and loose nightgown with no panties can be worn to indicate that she is not too bothered about foreplay. Black bra and panties means she wants to be "up on top."[7] When Kate Fillion describes all this as "preposterous,"[8] she is not alone.

Our next author, although a much better writer, also slides between nature and culture in a way similar to Gray. At times, his assumptions are that men and women are naturally different; at other times, he assumes their differences are due to "gender culture." But this author is not writing from a quasi-counseling perspective, and his intentions are not to reinforce patriarchal stereotypes. He is a novelist, humorist, and essayist, and his great gift is reflection on his own upbringing in the American Midwest. Garrison Keillor's amusing and witty volume, *The Book of Guys,* absorbs both these contradictory viewpoints simultaneously, moving from one to the other depending on which better

67

fits his illustration. Therefore, when he discusses male sexuality, he comes very close to sociobiology. He writes with his typical humor, "A monogamous man is like a bear on a bicycle. You can train him how to ride it. But he would rather be in the woods doing what all the other bears are doing."[9] His implication here is clear (although it is obviously tongue-in-cheek, and one never knows when to take Keillor seriously): Male sexuality is shaped by instincts and biological "needs" so that monogamy is "unnatural." Yet, on another page, he sees the differences between men and women not as the product of nature or essential sexual characteristics but as the product of gender culture. We are what we are because of the way gender attitudes and ideas have been communicated through our upbringing and expectations.

> Girls have it better from the beginning—don't kid yourself. They were allowed to play in the house where the books were and the adults and boys were sent outside like livestock—boys were noisy and rough and girls were nice so they got to stay and we had to go. Boys ran around in the yard with toy guns going "shwsh, shwsh" fighting wars for made up reasons and arguing about who was dead, whilst the girls stayed inside and played with dolls creating complex family groups and learning to solve problems through negotiation and role play. Which gender is better equipped to live an adult life would you guess? Is there any doubt about this? Is it even close?[10]

In his inimitable way, Keillor expresses what many feminist writers have also expressed: Wide-reaching gender differences have their origin in the cultural demarcations that were drawn between men and women in childhood. It is this, rather than biology, that affects how they now relate to each other in adulthood. And it is culture, too, that changes these attitudes over time and makes certain gender styles more acceptable. The problem comes when the culture of our upbringing collides with the culture of the day, when men are now required to be able to "bake a cherry pie, make melon balls and whip up a great soufflé."

Keillor can get away with whatever theoretical inconsistencies he holds because he is not writing as a theorist but as an entertainer and storyteller. In a popular and entertaining genre, he taps into some of the issues and ideas that have been bothering academics for several decades but that few academics can now make accessible. But he can also succeed in spite of inconsistencies because he brings the very ambiguities alive in his writing, and that is where his readers are. Most people are not clear whether men and women are created or constructed, and most people are unsure what they want men and women to be like. Keillor, therefore, engages all our sympathies when he describes the dual messages that women and men receive from each other. The new "acceptable" man is the one who can "converse easily about intimate matters, participate in recreational weeping, laugh, hug, be vulnerable. But next day go into work, place the bales into the barge and tote it."

The popularizing of the concept of difference has thus traveled far. It can be found in books on the psychology of gender, counseling manuals, popular educational handbooks, communication surveys, sociolinguistics, and contemporary film and television. British television sitcoms such as *Men Behaving Badly* explore what happens to a contemporary laddish culture when it operates in close proximity with women. The American show *Frasier* imagines what male-female relationships are like when orchestrated by a sensitized male psychologist. Gender difference is also the bread and butter of cartoonists. Even an artist as skillful as Gary Larson of *Far Side* draws on male fear of difference, with hilarious results. Advertisers play on male-female caricatures, sometimes overplaying them for effect.

69

Yet, some might feel that we have heard all this before. So much of the way the concept of difference is handled in the popular culture is not too dissimilar from the way it was handled in premodern days. Surely, comedians in music halls and men's drinking clubs have been earning good money trading on sexual differences and mother-in-law jokes for years. So what has changed? One thing is that women have entered the show. Women are articulating their own reading of these differences and whether as theorists, essayists, dramatists, or comedians are making their voices heard. It is women, too, who have made the more scholarly contributions, especially when the issues have not been seen from the perspective of the male as norm. This decision of women to speak for themselves has changed the structure of the debate and reflected it back from a different perspective.

Problems in Studying Gender Differences

When we move away from simplistic generalizations, however, it soon becomes clear that trying to identify key gender differences is a serious and more complex task than thinking about Mars and Venus might have led us to expect. It was easier when we could reduce everything to sex. This is partly because, in spite of the postmodern insistence that sex is as much a construction as gender, sex is a much easier category to work with than gender. Genetic, chromosomal, reproductive, and anatomical factors are all easy to identify and examine. We can see the differences in chromosomes by looking through the microscope. It is far more difficult to isolate gender factors in any detailed way because of their close relation with such other cultural factors as ethnicity, region, class, temperament, and age. In fact, when we look at any set of differences, we do not always know what script we are reading. In trying to understand masculinity, for example, we have to recognize that other features complicate the picture. Men from different cultures may diverge more greatly in how they react to a situation than a man and a woman from the same culture.

I saw an illustration of this some years ago when I was at a gathering of international students in Britain. I watched with great entertainment as two men, an Arab and an American, tried to hold a conversation with each other. In order for the Arab to have a decent conversation with the American, he had to stand very close to him, so he might speak comfortably in a low, intimate voice. But the American felt invaded by this kind of proximity. He needed space, distance, autonomy, safety, so he stepped backward and resumed his louder conversational style. The Arab looked puzzled, stepped forward, and tried to close the space to something more familial, close, and congenial. The American looked anxious and stepped back again. Then, slowly, step by step, the Arab maneuvered the American right across the room as each of them tried to find an appropriate distance from which they could comfortably carry on their conversation. The combination of gender and ethnic factors was very evident, but how would we evaluate which of these characteristics was due to gender and which to ethnicity?

Specific gender differences can also be difficult to identify because they are part of a cluster of cultural attitudes that change over time. When we try to give some sort of shape to the concepts "masculine" and "feminine," we also have to recognize that these are in a constant process of flux. In the early 1980s, for example, the British firm Mothercare published a sales catalog with a cover that would have been not only inappropriate but unthinkable in my father's generation. The cover showed a man with a bare chest holding two naked twin babies. The representation was clearly "masculine" rather than "feminine"; the twins were not held inward toward the breast, but were looking outward toward the viewer, free to gaze but with the security of a man's arms around them. The constructed meaning of the image was clear: Good fathers are those who offer both protection and intimacy to their offspring, and Mothercare is on the side of good fathers. The catalog was an enormous success, and the items of baby care enjoyed an increase in sales. Yet, it was a conception and a posture that would not have been acceptable as appropriate for a man in a previous generation.

Who responded to the catalog? Women, of course, for although the picture signified fatherhood, the target group was mothers. Mothers saw in this picture an icon of a father "bonding" with his children and embraced it as a positive image for relationships in their own families. Thirty years earlier it would have been regarded as offensive or even ridiculous, but it was now the epitome of sensitive masculinity and sold baby products. Ten years later the Mothercare image would probably not have had such success, and might even have been problematic again, due to widespread publicized incidents of child sexual abuse.

71

The category of gender is a responsive category: It changes in relation to other ideas or attitudes in both personal and public domains. We have to acknowledge that a multiplicity of factors combines to shape gender differences and their interpretations at any particular time. At this level, the postmodern deconstructionists are saying something crucial: If we reify gender and regard it as something fixed and definitive in the nature of relationships, we misunderstand it. We have to recognize that what is sometimes spoken of as gendered behavior is not simply gender-related but an interplay of many different social constructions. Furthermore, since the gender we are interested in is attached to people, we cannot ignore the interplay between gender characteristics and those of temperament or personality styles. If we do not acknowledge all of this, we simply reinforce stereotypes.

Since the popular books on the psychology of men and women largely fail to investigate any of these issues, where do we go for a more reliable analysis? The next chapter looks at some of the other options.

"DIFFERENCE" IN FEMINIST PSYCHOLOGY AND SOCIOLOGY

hankfully, there are people in between the postmodern scholars and the mass paperback writers. Over the last two decades, a number of researchers have done key work in the area of relationships. Although their approach is a long way from the philosophical analysis of Luce Irigaray and Rosi Braidotti, it is also in a different league from *Why Men Don't Iron* or *Men Are from Mars, Women Are from Venus.* Most of those I want to look at here are academics who, in a way similar to some of the feminist writers of the 1960s, have also made their work accessible to a popular audience. These scholars work in the areas of psychology, sociology, and linguistics.

The psychologists have produced a considerable portfolio of work over the years. American psychologist Carol Gilligan was comparing diverse traits in the psychology of men and women in the early 1980s, when many feminists were reluctant to consider them. Nancy Chodorow and Lillian Rubin were looking at male-female differences along post-Freudian lines but trying to explain them in developmental rather than sexual-biological terms.[1] Their work has influenced a generation of therapists. Lynne Segal has done pivotal work in sociology, especially in the sociology of masculinity. Her work is acknowledged by people of many other disciplines around the world.[2] These writers all have strong feminist sympathies and feel that women's lives can be improved only by engaging with differences rather than assuming sameness. Their work has been significant in helping people explore and identify differences, while at the same time refuse the conclusion that men and women are locked into two great camps and cannot be any other way. In many areas of thinking, what these scholars have said has become the new orthodoxy.

Another key contributor is the sociolinguist Deborah Tannen, professor of linguistics at Georgetown University in Washington, D.C., who presented her research in two books that have become best-sellers. Tannen was McGraw Distingished Lecturer at Princeton when she published *You Just Don't Understand: Women and Men in Conversation,* and her work is built on the starting point that although they are different, women and men have equally valid conversational styles. In her preface she explains why, in spite of her intention, some women remain suspicious of the emphasis on difference. She echoes the fears that Jean Joseph Goux expressed, although more concretely:

> Some women fear, with justification, that any observation of gender differences will be heard as implying that it is women who are different—different from the standard which is whatever men are. The male is seen as normative, the female as departing from the norm. And it is only a short step—maybe an inevitable one—from different to "worse."[3]

Tannen is aware that the bid for equality has held previous feminist scholars back from considering and naming differences. She is in sympathy with "those who wish there were no differences between women and men—only reparable social injustice."[4] She has little time for biological essentialism, placing her own emphasis clearly in the cultural category. She also sees the dangers of reductionism whenever women and men are divided into two categories and generalizations are presented. Given these reservations, why then has she opted for "difference" in her own analysis of gender communication? Her answer is straightforward: Because difference is there. Denying it can "only compound the confusion that is already widespread in the era of shifting and re-forming relationships between women and men."[5]

Feminist writers are not the only ones who have looked at differences while developing critiques of essentialism. Although it was clearly in women's interests to attack bad theories, particularly ones that left women with so few practical options, male scholars have also entered the debate. They did so not merely to show solidarity with women but to engage with their own agendas in various studies of masculinity. Similar questions about identity and gender relations have become the subject of a number of studies by men psychologists, social scientists, and theologians. Stuart Miller wrote a book on male friendship,[6] Robert Bly invited men to be initiated anew into the world of the father, Reuben Fine tried to get men to rediscover the forgotten male psyche, and Roy McCloughry examined masculinity from a Christian perspective. The resulting volumes are diverse in a similar way to the studies done by women writers. Australian psychologist David Tacey notes this in his book *Remaking Men*. He argues that there is now a widening gulf between the feminist-influenced "critical" writing that seeks to destabilize patriarchal masculinity and the Jungian-inspired "popular" writing that seeks to promote a "new-old" masculinity. He is profoundly critical of the traditional biological reductionism present in much Jungian orthodoxy and expressed in this example by Eugene Monick:

75

> Males and females are significantly different anatomically and biologically. It is my assumption that from these differences certain distinctions have evolved into the psychological characteristics of masculinity and femininity. The characteristics are gender-specific since their basis is biological: they are instinctual and archetypal.[7]

Monick feels it is time to leave this behind and to "remake masculinity." Not least is the need "to differentiate the new self-esteem from the old masculinist arrogance, to separate the new happiness from the old complacency, to tell the differences between human rights and patriarchal privileges."[8]

Differences in Relationship and Friendship Patterns

In these studies in sociology, psychology, and sociolinguistics, the most reliable research has yielded a surprising level of agreement on what constitutes the key differences in the way men and women function and relate. Without trying to apportion "weightings" to various cultural or genetic factors, various descriptions and analyses of difference recur. Broadly summarizing, men and women are said to demonstrate different ways of interacting, expressing emotions, playing games, having a conversation, handling authority, giving and receiving instructions, initiating friendships, reacting to problems, establishing connections, relating to hierarchies, appraising situations, and taking control. Sometimes this is seen as evidence that men and women orient themselves differently toward reality. Men are more likely to be separate, individualistic, oppositional, and to think in terms of binaries, whereas women show greater "connectedness" and orient themselves empathetically toward others. This conclusion is similar to that of Luce Irigaray and Helene Cixous, although with different philosophical underpinnings.

One way to examine some of these differences is by looking at studies on friendship. It is generally suggested that men have much greater difficulty forming intimate relationships than women. This conclusion is reinforced by Stuart Miller in his study of male friendship in America. He suggests that "men may have wives, they may even have women friends, but their relationships with other men are generally characterised by thinness, insincerity, and even chronic wariness." Another writer suggests that relationships between men "do not call for high levels of self-disclosure nor its reciprocal—trust." Consequently, "female friendships are both more exclusive and more emotionally committed than male friendships."[9]

Now that many men have come together in groups, specifically committed to exploring male friendships and intimacy, it is fruitful to look at the evidence they produce. One author who participates in a men's group documented the complexity of developing relationships that are noncompetitive and emotionally open. A particular incident is telling. After a meeting, this author was walking through the parking lot with a member of the group who had been helped back to emotional health after a bad period. Arriving at his car, the man stopped, and making full eye contact with his friend, told him, "I just want you to know that I love you." The man who told the story said that in spite of all they had done together in the group, at this disclosure, the hairs on the back of his neck stood up and a great shiver ran down his spine. Muttering something fast, he made a bid to escape. Talking to me afterward, he wondered how differently we might have reacted had the incident happened between two women. For my part I felt fairly confident that I would not have felt threatened by such a disclosure of love, fearing it neither as a sexual overture nor as an invasion of my "ego boundaries." My response would more likely have been to accept her declaration of love and hug her in response!

Due to many stories similar to this, those involved in gender research generally accept that whereas women relate easily to each other concerning experiences and feelings, male friends find it difficult to give or receive intimate self-disclosure. They connect more easily through impersonal issues such as ideas, sports, work, and politics. One characteristic method of studying differences in friendship patterns is to ask married men and women to name their six best friends. Typically, women find it difficult to write down the names of six friends because they would rather write down seven or eight. They have to do some negotiating to decide whom to leave out. Husbands may or may not be included on the list, although their exclusion does not imply they are insignificant in the lives of their wives. It is rather that women define friends differently. When the men find the task difficult, however, it is more likely because they usually do not have six friends to name, and their wife might feature as the first (and sometimes only) person on their list.[10] If such differences in the way women and men relate exist, why do they occur? And if what Miller says is true, what is the explanation for the "thinness and wariness" of male friendships in cultures of North European origin?

Explaining Difference

Some writers link friendship differences to differences in attitudes toward vulnerability. Whereas woman have the "emotional space" to show vulnerability, men do not, for vulnerability in men is perceived as inappropriate weakness. Although it is now acceptable for a man to express his vulnerable feelings to a woman, it remains more dangerous for him to show vulnerability to another man. And since close friendship cannot develop between people who are guarded and covered with protective layers, it is clearly easier for women to develop close relationships than it is for men. To name the problem as a fear of vulnerability, however, is simply to offer another symptom, not an explanation, for it begs the additional question, What lies behind that?

Another answer relates these different patterns to the development of gender culture in the public and private arenas. Men have been segregated into work patterns and work environments where they have been required to be competitive, successful, and individualists. (And as psychologists tell us regularly, "Isolated, competing egos do not easily open up their hearts to each other."[11]) On the other hand, women have been given permission to spend more time with children and other mothers in shared patterns of child care and away from competitive work. Therefore, they can disclose their emotions, vulnerability, and weaknesses with other women with relatively little loss of face.

The problem with this explanation is that the differences in relationship are evident before men and women ever enter the workforce or become parents. Like many mothers, I had a chance to observe early stages of male-female friendship patterns as I waited for my three sons to finish school each day. Often if it was sunny, and since my preschooler wanted to see his older brother playing, I would arrive early, during the mid-afternoon break, and watch the different activities of the girls and the boys. Although some changes took place over the many years I watched by the school gates, some things remained very much the same. When the play space was not segregated, the youngsters making most of the noise and creating most of the activity were inevitably boys. They would race around the playground chasing various shapes of balls, usually arguing about who should pass the ball to

78

whom, whether a goal had been scored, and who was winning. Nothing ever seemed obvious: All of these were opportunities for disagreement. The boys who were not involved in the communal activity that took up so much space in the yard were often isolated and looked very much on their own.

Some girls were involved in running, but their games were more likely to be less rough and noisy, and they each had a turn. More likely, however, the girls went around in small groups or in twos. Girls had "best friends," and the way they expanded their circle was often by running up to a third girl and saying, "Do you want to share a secret?" or, more inquisitively, "Do you know a secret?" The sharing of the secret would allow a third or fourth person into the intimacy, creating a bond, a closeness. Not that this intimacy was always cozy. Sometimes I would notice a new constellation of girls, with a former best friend now isolated. As the girls ran to me, a regular landmark, to share their news (Charlotte had a new baby brother, Kate's grandma had moved, Petra had a birthday), I would point to a girl on her own and ask, "But what's the matter with Lisa?" The answer was often a kind of denial: "Oh, she doesn't want to play." Then Lisa's former best friend would run off with her arm tucked in another's, whispering conspiratorially. Boys were as ready to cut others out too and usually in a much more overt way, often decided by physical features ("He's too fat to be on the team," or, "He's too little to be goalie."), but much of their activity was subject to the larger objective rather than to their relationships with each other. The boys on the receiving end of the "shut out" also found that girls were not likely to respect them either.

By pushing gender differences further and further back into childhood, it is difficult to argue that the causes are to be found in an adult cultural context. Some writers, particularly Nancy Chodorow and Carol Gilligan, have suggested that we would have to go a long way back to understand the power and force of these differences. Women and men are oriented in different ways toward reality because there is some patterning in their very psyche that draws them in these directions.

However, even though Chodorow would argue for differences at this very basic level, she would not buy into any part of essentialist biology. Arguing from attachment theory, she links these differences of orientation not to anatomy but to psychosocial development. She maintains that they are related to emotions, which occur early in the conscious/unconscious development of small children. Especially significant is a boy's need to "separate" from his mother, to find his own emotionality and sexuality, which a girl, being the same sex, does not need to do.

According to developmental psychology, the formation of identity involves two key processes: bonding and detachment. Both girls and boys experience attachment to the mother as the primary care giver. And the main way a girl can acquire a sense of self is by continuing the attachment or bond with her mother, who in turn identifies with her daughter. She is the same sex as her mother and can find her identity in that similarity. As a result, suggests Chodorow, girls grow up with their primary definition of self permeated with a basis of empathy. Being feminine can mean being and feeling connected to others, and ego boundaries are fluid and permeable. For a boy, however, the process is different. To develop his identity as a man, he needs to relinquish his bond and attachment to his mother. Because he is different from her, he cannot identify with her. Therefore, a boy's gender identity is created by emotional separation.[12] His ego boundaries are more fixed and definite, and he has to work out his own identity in relation to his father, which is why fathering is such an important activity with reference to sons. Consequently, as adults, men fear closeness, for it threatens their sense of separate identity, while women fear isolation and aloneness, for it threatens theirs. Gilligan sums it up: "Since masculinity is defined through separation while femininity is defined through attachment, male gender identity is threatened by intimacy while female gender identity is threatened by separation." According to Gilligan, women speak in unison "in a different voice." Women's concern involves empathizing and showing care, whereas men's concerns are based on abstract principles of justice and fairness.[13]

The way males and females form their identity has implications in many areas of male-female relationships. For example, there are differences in what men and women say they most dislike about each other's attitudes. When they are not shown respect, women feel indignant, but men experience it as a crisis of identity. Men are also more likely than women to be highly sensitive to what they experience as an apparent lack of respect and to interpret certain responses as a put-down. Such attitudes are reflected in problems within intimate relationships. Most men feel annoyed if their sexual advances are rebuffed, for such actions attack their "ego identity," whereas women feel distressed when they do not feel cherished, since that undermines theirs.

The separateness/connectedness divide is very significant in intimacy and sexual expression. Psychologists such as James Olthuis have pointed out that for many men with strong ego boundaries, emotional closeness is relatively hard to come by. Often, then, sex is the only permissible route available to emotional warmth and expression. Consequently, because these men experience sex as the main component of tenderness, deep feelings themselves become sexualized, and affection, protectiveness, and feelings of gratitude often become entangled with sexual attraction. For most women, differentiation is much easier because they have traditionally been allowed a wider range of emotional responses and expressions. As a consequence of this, many women need emotional warmth and affection before they can commit themselves sexually. Many men, on the other hand, feel they need sex before they can let go of their inhibitions and draw close. This may be evident in marriage itself. Sometimes when a man finds it difficult to be demonstrative or emotionally in tune with his wife, sex is the way in which he is able to express his affection and love for her. It is easy for a wife to misunderstand this, however, and feel she is merely an object. It is also a problem for women for whom emotional closeness is usually a prerequisite to full sexual enjoyment.[14]

DIFFERENCE HAS ITS CONTEMPORARY CRITICS

Needless to say, those who embrace strong concepts of difference, not least both Gilligan and Chodorow, have their critics.[15] Some challenge their process of theorizing. Arguing from some alleged pretheoretical attachment crisis produces a thesis that is simply untestable. How do we know that boys face this problem of separation, which results in such strong psychical factors? These theorists are simply reading it back from currently observed criteria. Others point out that this is yet another form of essentialism, and one not far from the biological reductionism it is trying to replace. What does it matter whether "difference" has its origin in *sexual* difference or in contrasting patterns of emotional attachment to mother that *follow* from sexual difference? Surely, either way, sex still lies at the bottom of it. And when we give such a significant role to biology, to then "explain" gender differences in relationships in terms of attachment theory is simply an "add on."

Others blame these theorists for romanticizing female empathy and connectedness, which always seems to give women the moral high ground and sees men as ineffectual relaters.[16] The terms of the debate are already loaded, argues Kate Fillion, who challenges the identification of disclosure with intimacy:

> Men who say they demonstrate affection by doing things for others typically get low ratings on intimacy scales, women who say they demonstrate affection by telling others about their feelings get high ratings. Men tell researchers that they do feel close to their friends, and show it through "mutual give and take," "helping each other out," "being there for each other" and sharing "activities." Not good enough many experts say: only mutual self-disclosure counts as real closeness.[17]

Fillion's book attempts to refute notions that have become vogue, and she simultaneously attacks the popular and scholarly writings for propagating ideas of difference and thereby downplaying both similarity and equality. She refuses the "truisms" that "women love, men lust; women want relationships, men fear intimacy; women are nurturing, men are aggressive."[18] She believes that women collude in perpetuating their own powerlessness and unhappiness when they promote theories that men and women are psychological opposites. Her own conclusion is that we must continue to do what we have been doing for thirty years—debunk the old gender myths that reinforce inequality and resist the new myths about women that "we are more-than-equal when it comes to caring, sharing and keeping the peace, and we are more spiritual than sexual in the boardroom, the bedroom and every place in between."[19] It seems that equality and sameness are not yet moribund, not even in psychology.

In spite of these important points of criticism, the Chodorow thesis cannot be dismissed too quickly. Locating "difference" in our emotional development may not be testable in a positivistic sense, yet it does offer a useful framework for understanding some of the factors about male-female relationships that are otherwise inexplicable. And it is different from a bald biological reductionism in that it gives much space to other factors and scope for change. Many therapists have observed, for example, that young men who have had close relationships with their fathers are often better at intimate relationships than those who have not. According to the Chodorow thesis, this makes sense. Incorporating fathers into detailed early infant care would make "separation" from mother much less of a crisis for the male psyche. The argument holds up under many examples, but, like any theory, it is partial, and the full story remains to be told.

GENDER AND COMMUNICATION

If the work of psychologists of difference raises such strong objections, the work of sociolinguist Deborah Tannen has met with wide approval partly because her style is nonjudgmental and linked less to psychological theory than to a broad idea of gender culture. For Tannen, boys and girls grow up in different worlds of words. Boys relate to groups that are hierarchically structured, girls to friendship pairs. These differences provide the context in which men and women learn to listen and talk. Tannen's writing has different philosophical justifications from the work of the other theorists. Her approach is more empirical; she offers observations, stories of male-female communication, and then an interpretative reading. Her work is successful because many couples are able to relate it to their own communication patterns.

83

Her basic premise, that gender culture deeply affects how we learn to communicate, can be tested by anyone. My own experiences illustrate it. I was brought up in postwar Yorkshire, England, and many of my early experiences of conversation involved listening to my mother and her sisters. When they met, one of them would begin the conversation immediately, usually while removing her coat. I soon recognized that this was a way to seize the conversation while she had the chance, otherwise another sister would get the first word and would

be difficult to stop! The brief "solo" would be punctuated by inter-
ruptions and agreements by the others, until at some stage or another,
they would all be talking at once. Many of the rules of conversation
were conveyed to me in these early days. For example, I learned from
the age of four that it was extremely discourteous to allow someone
to finish a sentence! You had to finish it for them, or interrupt, just to
show that you were listening. Throughout my young adulthood,
female communication was always a group activity, accompanied by
noises of affirmation, body gestures, exclamations, and nods of support. Empathetic listening was the most crucial ingredient in any discourse. Consequently, when I married my husband, a man from the
South of England, the silence surrounding our conversations was a
culture shock. In our first few months, I would ask him regularly, "Are
you listening to me?" His measured response was, "Yes, that is why I
am not talking."

Tannen builds up dozens of examples of the different expectations
men and women have in conversation. It is not only that men give
and receive information and women relate empathetically. Differences
also exist in the way they read tones, gestures, and intentions. Both
men and women listen "beneath" the conversation, but they pick up
different things. Men are more likely to pick up condescension; women
are more likely to hear anxiety or concern. Because so much of their
own conversation is goal-related and functional, men may also be hard
pressed to "understand" much of women's conversation and sit there
waiting for them to "get to the point." For most women, on the other
hand, the conversation *is* the point.

Due to these and a host of other differences, women and men can
simply miss each other in communication and not know why the other
seems frustrated. To offer another personal example, I thought communication in my own marriage had greatly improved as time went
on, which is why it came as a surprise when after nearly twenty years
of married life my husband pointed out that I hardly ever actually
answered his questions. On that day, we were expecting a visitor, and
I was traveling to lecture in a city a hundred miles away. Alan had just
asked me what time my lecture began. I replied by pointing out that
it would be very difficult to stay to see his visitor, for I would miss the
early train and the late one was unreliable. My husband said that as

usual I hadn't answered his question. I denied it: I had given a perfectly good answer. He disagreed: He had asked a question about the lecture time, and I had made up a much more complicated question about trains and a visitor and answered that. He was right! After some thought, I realized why this was. I couldn't believe he really wanted an answer to such a mundane inquiry, so I went "beneath" it to what I assumed was the real question, namely, could I stay to see the visitor and still get to the lecture. I translated the question and produced the answer that satisfied me, instead of simply supplying him with what he had asked for. When he insisted that he had simply been interested in knowing the time of my lecture, with no ulterior motive, I could not (and still cannot!) understand why. It simply seemed to be pointless information!

QUESTIONING ASSUMPTIONS

The contemporary interest in difference rather than sameness is not, for the most part, a return to premodern attitudes. To accept the existence of difference as a virtually incontrovertible fact no longer entails buying into biological essentialism. We can consider other sources for it. Postmodern writers have certainly broken this link, but so have others. The psychologists, sociologists, and sociolinguists we have looked at all work with metanarratives, for example the desirability of justice and mutuality and the belief that general explanations are possible. They also accept difference without essentialist overtones. From this position, it is possible to maintain that human beings and human societies can change. One of the aims of change is to explore how better relationships can be achieved. The consensus seems to be that they have to be achieved without stereotyping differences that exist between women and men and without abandoning them either.

Theorists in the social sciences inevitably write from philosophical assumptions, sometimes overtly so, but few of them have explored any of the key *theological* questions implicit in this discussion. This is a pity because a dialogue between theology and the social sciences could be both fruitful and exciting. Theologians are often reticent to take this on because the social sciences have developed from within a secularist framework for over a century and contain assumptions and approaches that theologians find difficult to deal with. Social scientists do not take this on because most of them are agnostic if not atheistic about the existence of God and do not believe that a study of theology holds much relevance for their work. Another reason for the lack of dialogue is that theology has had its own battles and has hardly led the way in advancing significant research in the area of sex and gender. In the next chapter I turn to some theological issues and ask why theologians have not been more involved in the creation-construction debate.

From Social Science
to Theology

I f books on postmodern feminism are not widely sought after by
the general public, books on academic theology have an equally
limited audience. Yet, as in popular psychology, writings in popular theology have proliferated in the area of sex and gender, and
like their secular counterparts, they contain a jumbled confusion
of perspectives. There is a difference, however. Most of these books
claim to offer "Christian" insights—telling the truth about men and
women as God has created them and designed them to be. Sadly,
though, too many of them rehash old ideas based on biological essentialism plus gender stereotypes and support them with biblical quo-
tations taken out of context. Such arguments, unfortunately, serve to
reinforce the connection between Christianity and an unexamined
premodernity in the eyes of many critics.

During most of its history, theological interest in issues of sexuality has been limited to the areas of sexual ethics, the doctrine of "man"
(Christian anthropology), and pastoralia. Even within these areas,

gender has rarely been a separate part of the discourse. Usually it has been subsumed under "sex" or hidden under what some people called "masculine headship." There were rumblings of inquiry in earlier centuries as some mystics tried to find a spirituality that addressed them specifically as women, and some branches of the church tried to develop a theology that was overtly inclusive of men and women. The Reformation provided a new impetus with its embracing concept of the "priesthood of all believers." But a full discussion of sex and gender was not to take place until the late twentieth century. When it did take place, it was not only issues in Christian anthropology, sexual ethics, and pastoralia that were the focus. It was the entire process of theologizing itself, for the key issue in this new critical theology was not about finding space for a discussion of sex and gender within the existing discourse. Rather, it was whether theology itself was an irretrievably gendered discipline in which its language, concepts, arguments, and assumptions were inherently masculine.

THE THEOLOGICAL CONTEXT

Before we move into this current debate, we need to step back and see it in relation to the structure and history of theological inquiry, for as an academic discipline, theology has had a much longer history than the social sciences, which did not appear on the scene until after the Enlightenment. Until the entrenched secularism of the late twentieth century, the study of theology had always been an integral part of the curriculum of Western education. Not that it was ever simply seen as just another academic discipline. People had never regarded theology as a neutral or objective science in the way in which some scientists and mathematicians claimed objectivity for their disciplines. Now, of course, it is widely conceded that even in the most rigorous of scientific areas, axioms and assumptions of a fundamental philosophical nature provide a starting point for the very analysis and accumulation of knowledge.

This issue is not remarkable for theologians. Christian theology has always been fairly overt about its starting point, which is that the meaning of life, if there is one, lies beyond the boundaries of most of our

88

sensory knowledge and experience. I say "if there is one" because today many theologians are happy to do theology without addressing the vexing question of whether they believe it or not. (This came home to me in a discussion with some theologians who trained people for Christian ministry. When someone asked if we could formulate, as a working document, a statement of faith to which we might assent, the question was met with hesitation. When two reluctant colleagues were pressed for some credal affirmation, one of them offered tentatively, "I can say I hope there is a God.")

By and large, theology has been built on more than vague hope that there is a God; it has proceeded from the tacit but widespread acknowledgment that if indeed God exists, then we have an obligation to know something about God. We also need to consider the question as to whether human life itself can be understood except in relation to God. For those reasons alone, as well as for the historical and literary interest of the material, the study of biblical texts, doctrine, and history is deemed important. They give us a way of understanding both the nature of faith and the content of what Christians believe. This does not mean, however, that the study of theology has ever been a simple task. On the contrary, a large number of philosophical perspectives, historical influences, traditions, and interpretations have always been part of the development and shape of the discipline. Each of these in turn has left its legacy on the contemporary theological discussion of sex and gender.

89

Scripture and Tradition

The central focus of Christian theology has been the Christian Scriptures, the Old and New Testaments. Yet, theologians are not simply biblical exegetes. They also investigate what some generally refer to as the "tradition of the church," grappling with issues of history, philosophy, doctrine, and canonical authority in the context of the historic creeds and councils. There is an ongoing question in theology about the relationship between tradition and Scripture, a question that is both subtle and intricate. Some argue that Scripture cannot be seen except as a part of tradition, and therefore, is subject to tradition (which in Catholicism usually means the *magisterium*) for its interpretation. What are the Scriptures other than those books ratified by a council of the early church? "Tradition" first drew up the Canon and decided what constituted the Bible. It was within the tradition, from the church fathers onward, that the doctrines of the church were first articulated in its creeds, catechisms, and confessions. The Nicene Creed, the Thirty-Nine Articles, the Westminster Confession, the Heidelberg Catechism, and all the other historic formularies that contain the basic affirmations of what Christians believe are not found in Scripture but are the products of the church's reflection on Scripture, which then become embedded in our theology.

Others insist that the Scriptures themselves are the yardstick for tradition. The Canon might have been ratified by men, but the books in the Canon were inspired by the Holy Spirit of God as the touchstone for our faith. The creeds articulate the teachings of the bibical Christian faith in summary form. Tradition itself has to be held up against the teachings of Scripture to ensure that orthodoxy prevails. That is how we develop concepts of orthodoxy and heresy. Heresy is the name given to any tradition that departs from biblical teaching and therefore cannot be regarded as authentic. What the councils of the church have always done, whether at Jerusalem, Alexandria, Nicea, Geneva, or Heidelberg, is to look at what has become embedded as tradition and ask, "Is this truly biblical?" Where error has crept in, it has been necessary to revise tradition and represent it to the church.

90

Philosophy

The study of theology is also affected by other philosophical perspectives and assumptions, which have traveled through the centuries. Philosophy has always played a major role in theology, even though the extent of that influence may be unacknowledged or even unrecognized. Greek philosophy (which itself was influenced by a pagan culture) has influenced theology for two thousand years. The legacy of the debate between the Platonists and the Aristotelians has been passed down through the centuries and is found today in colleges throughout the United States, so that people in the various churches who may never have read either Plato or Aristotle could still be affected by them in their own understanding of the faith. Similarly, Kantian idealism, Cartesian dualism, British empiricism, Hegelian antithesis, utilitarianism, European existentialism, and even the works of Ludwig Wittgenstein have all had an impact on the way we approach theology today. The "Sea of Faith" movement is a product of its time: It could have begun only at the end of the second millennium.

Culture and Context

Finally, other prevailing cultural ideas also influence the study of theology. The Scriptures themselves were given to specific cultures and are read today in other cultures. Those who read the Scriptures must always weigh what has contemporary significance. The culture of our societies provides both the context in which we think about God and also the material conditions through which we think about God. Current societal values play into our theologizing and what we deem to be significant or appropriate discourse. Theology done in Britain in the seventeenth century needed to relate to the beginnings of modern science in a way that was different from theology done in North Africa in the third century. Liberation theology comes out of Latin America in the twentieth century not out of Massachusetts in the eighteenth, even though the same biblical texts were available at both times.

In some particularly conservative colleges of theology, there is such understandable wariness about the extent to which "external" influences have dominated the development of theology that the discipline itself is often approached with suspicion. Some theologians are concerned that theology has become sterile, dry, and formulaic, involving too much spurious and academic debate. In an attempt to counter its potentially negative influence, they choose to limit their own inquiry largely to biblical studies, systematics, and ethics (which is seen as "applied biblical studies"). This way, it is felt, they can at least achieve some objectivity and definiteness as they ground their faith on a firm foundation and agreed basis of authority. Yet, this retreat can be dangerous. It hides the fact that we can never escape our own human limitations and our cultural and historical location. When the biblical texts themselves have to be read, understood, and applied within a context that is inevitably different from the contexts into which they were first given, a process of interpretation and extrapolation inevitably

91

takes place. Even the most pious or scholarly should beware of becoming overly confident and insisting they can always grasp and present the truth without any kind of error.

Reading the Bible

We therefore never read Scripture "neutrally." We always bring to the biblical text our own minds, perspectives, ideas, attitudes, location, history, culture, nuances, and concerns that are all, themselves, extra-scriptural. We also absorb biblical teaching in the context of our own embodied situation as persons, with regional, ethnic, and gendered differences. There is nothing new about this. People have approached Scripture this way through the centuries, which is why the Bible has been such a powerful catalyst for cultural change. It can speak to every situation with challenges relevant for that time and location, nourishing movements for reform within church and society. Many have pointed out that a "biblical worldview" lies beneath our seventeenth-century concept of law, our development of science, political democracy, and honest and accountable public service.

Yet, because we approach the Bible from our different locations, we can also find ourselves in disagreement. It is quite possible to be completely committed to faith in God and to reading the Scriptures yet still sometimes be trapped by our own philosophical assumptions of which we are unaware. So even when people agree that the Bible offers truth (and we also need to define and explore what we mean by truth, for it sometimes has a historical referent, sometimes linguistic, legal, propositional, parabolic, narrative, didactic, biographic, or prophetic, all of which are modalities through which truth is received and understood), they do not necessarily agree on what that truth is. We can also still get it wrong. Our understanding, exegesis, interpretation, and application of Scripture are, sadly, even among the best of us prone to error, which is inevitable, for in spite of our best efforts, we, unfortunately, are not omniscient. We are not God. We are limited finite beings with finite human minds often imprisoned in limited ways of understanding the world. Although God speaks truth into our human condition, our human condition means we do not always receive it.

At this point, it seems important to clarify what I am not saying. I am not offering this series of qualifications and cautions as a justification for either agnosticism or relativism. Nor am I suggesting that we are forever doomed to provisionality and approximation. Postmodernity is difficult to square with committed Bible study. I have no interest in siding with the "liberal" claim that those who are committed to certainty are *ipso facto* arrogant and presumptuous. To hold on to a belief in the authority of a Creator God, the destructive power of sin, the atoning work of Christ, and the empowerment of the Holy Spirit is not arrogance. It is nothing more than acknowledgment of the Christian faith. I am not countering fervently held belief in any way but simply pressing for a little humility, for humility is an essential ingredient in the task of theology. As with any students or scholars, theologians are servants not masters (or mistresses) of what they study. Once we claim infallible authority on biblical interpretation, then we have already ceased to see ourselves as human and have claimed divinity.

Therefore, we need to examine constantly the assumptions that we bring to any reading of the Bible, and some of those assumptions are related to sex and gender. In striving to be biblical, we may be merely cultural. We may be merely holding some of the pervading, unexamined attitudes and ideas about the relationship between men and women and then unconsciously imposing them upon Scripture. This again is nothing new. Many of our biblical commentaries contain observations that we now know are more related to prevailing cultural ideas than to the real teachings of Scripture. Biblical translation itself can even be affected. In an attempt to make the text clear, the result can be as much an interpretation of the actual words as a translation.

An obvious example of this comes in St. Paul's letter to the Romans (16:1). He sends the letter with Phoebe and urges the church to welcome her and give her warm recognition. Yet our translations deprive us of the full impact of what Paul says. Paul refers to Phoebe in Greek as *diokonos* (with not even a feminization of the ending), and in the next verse as *prostatis* (normally "leader"). Yet, when translated into English, for years she has been given the status "servant of the church"

93

and "helper." There may be some exegetical justification for this weaker translation of *prostatis,* but not for *diokonos.* Thomas Schreiner defends the translation rather lamely: "Many think that Phoebe is called a deacon in Romans 16:1. It should be noted, however, that the word *diokonos . . .* is often a general term and thus one cannot be sure that Phoebe was a deacon."[1] This is true, for the same term is applied to both Paul and Timothy, whose ministries were different from those we associate with the office of deacon.

The point is, however, the partiality of the translation. The translators have cut out certain meanings and have translated the same word quite differently when it is used elsewhere. When Paul applies the word *diokonos* to his own calling, or when it is used to describe Timothy, it assumes a "higher" status in translation than when it is used of Phoebe. No one doubts that Paul's diaconal calling meant that he was set apart as a minister of the gospel. So why was this same translation not used in Phoebe's case, even though Paul had used the same description of service that he applied to himself? Why rather than being called "deacon" is she simply called "servant"? It can only be because the translators did not believe Paul meant it! They had to make sure we understand that Phoebe, as a woman, could not possibly have been a deacon in the same sense as Paul or any other man. They, therefore, speak for Paul, nailing down the meaning and depriving us, incidentally, of recognizing the courtesy and gratitude Paul accords to this woman's ministry.[2] Biblical studies may be "safer" than theology, but reading the Bible still leaves us prone to the same philosophical assumptions we bring to the study of theology.

We can see that the questions of sex and gender in theology occur at several levels. They come at the level of tradition itself, where the past practices of the church, its government, its leadership patterns, and its liturgy have taken up positions on men and women that need to be addressed. They also occur at the level of Scripture: Are we basing our tradition, our practices, and, indeed, our theology on a wise interpretation of Scripture, or are we distorting the message in some way? Questions come, too, at the level of influences. How much do we take prevailing cultural ideas or arguments into our own mind-set (including ideas of biology and roles) and then overlay them with theological justification? Finally, they occur at the level of power and privilege.

To what extent are the decisions made by the powerful in the church influenced by the very fact of their own power? And if this is the case, in what way is this means of decision making different from any secular pattern of patriarchy? These are some of the questions that will occupy the next chapter.

SEX AND GENDER IN THEOLOGY: THE PREMODERN PROBLEM

With the same caveats and qualifications I offered earlier, I want to introduce Jean Joseph Goux's distinction between premodern, modern, and postmodern into the theological discourse on sexuality. The concept "premodern" would characterize most of the discussion as it has been formed by the traditions of the church. Certainly, one might say (as I suggested earlier) that there is an unavoidable premodernity whenever one talks of our humanness as derivative. If we are brought into being by a Creator, and thereby dependent on that Creator for our existence, we have already come down on one side of the creation-construction debate. Yet, we can still hold that our sexuality is put into the creation by God and recognize that our differences might also be developmental and cultural. Unfortunately, there is little acknowledgment of this in the premodern mentality.

PREMODERNITY IN A THEOLOGY OF THE SEXES

For many theological writers throughout the centuries, "difference" has been seen as total, almost deterministic. It maps out our relative place in reality. It decides what God has created men and women for, recognizes what sins we are responsible for, determines what roles we may play, and judges what gifts we may exercise. A premodern perspective in theology carries with it a welter of assumptions that interpret difference as all-embracing; it is the God-ordained structure of human identity through which we are given our functions, feelings, place, and perceptions. It even encompasses our spirituality.

There is no shortage of evidence for this view. Any study of the early church fathers will unearth misogynous comments that show a great gap in the way men and women were perceived. This is often in spite of some wonderful insights into the nature of the Trinity and love. Alongside a justifiable emphasis on the dangers of sin and evil is an unjustifiable emphasis on women as the ones responsible for most of it. Women were regularly blamed for the weight of evil in the world. The fathers variously described women as "the devil's gateway,"[1] "misbegotten men,"[2] or "a temple built over a sewer."[3]

In a climate of asceticism, women's difference from men, their sexuality, was deeply problematic. To put it bluntly, women's sexuality was a fundamental problem, a snare of the devil to draw men away from purity into lust. The austere St. Jerome was so anxious about sexual difference that he urged his women followers to pursue a way of life that made them as unattractive as possible, to do penance and ensure that their difference could not be noticed. A truly spiritual woman would be "squalid with dirt, almost blind with weeping . . . continence . . . her luxury, her life a fast."[4] He also brought some of his anxieties about women's sexuality, even about its expression in marriage, into biblical exegesis itself, claiming an uncleanness about anything that was "coupled." Anything that denoted female difference from the male, even the number two, was

98

for Jerome profoundly threatening and therefore must illustrate God's own displeasure:

> There is something not good in the number 2 . . . while scripture on the first, third, fourth and sixth days relates that having finished the works of each God saw that it was good, on the second day He omitted this altogether, leaving us to understand that 2 is not a good number because it prefigures the marriage contract.[5]

Although these worst excesses of a premodern mentality belong to history and not to contemporary Christianity, these attitudes have not altogether departed, either from biblical exegesis or from the attitudes of churchmen. In 1985, the Anglican High Churchman William Oddie wrote *What Will Happen to God?* a book that gives an apocalyptic vision of what will happen to Christian truth if fundamental differences between women and men are not heeded in our practices. He pictures a domino effect, in which one piece (for example, the revision of gender-exclusive language) will topple the whole of the Christian edifice and disaster will follow.

The problem is that Oddie's book is littered with unexamined concepts, uninvestigated assumptions, and thin hermeneutics. His analysis leans heavily on secular stereotypes that sound much like Gray or Moir on popular psychology. He insists, for example, that "modern industrial culture is one in which the male (with his generally greater aggression, 'goal-orientation,' 'visual-spatial ability') is particularly suited."[6] At the same time he gives a maternal, spiritual task to women, for they are to "protect the world and men like a mother, and purify life as the Virgin."[7] For him, women's difference not only disqualifies them from performing tasks that have traditionally fallen to men, including leadership in the church, it also puts them on a different religious plane. Oddie has some doubtful things indeed to say about the relation between spirituality and sexuality. He makes the extraordinary claim that "it is a clear and consistent biblical assumption that . . . biological differences (of men and women) correspond to clear differences of spiritual identity." He attempts to substantiate this, however, not by reflecting on Scripture but by offering the same point again as an anthropological explanation: "In all societies, this

99

perception of an essentially spiritual, as well as merely biological difference between the sexes has been reflected in a clear delineation of their social roles and in distinct ways of behaving."[8]

The argument is circular, yet it is sincerely held. Here is a classical exposition of a premodern view of difference: fixed, immutable, God-given. The whole of male-female reality is permeated by differences that are reflected in biology, roles, and spiritual identity. These differences also bar women from the priesthood: Priests are representatives of Christ. Christ was male. Therefore, quite simply, it is impossible for a woman to perform the priestly act as Christ's representative. They have the wrong kind of genitals. (There is a shift in concept here, of course, from being Christ's "representative" to being Christ's "representation" [i.e., to look like him], but that usually gets lost in the passion of feeling.) One opponent of the ordination of women sums it up baldly: "When men can have babies, women can be ordained."

We are more likely to find these arguments offered from a more Catholic perspective (and, indeed, Oddie left the Church of England for the Roman Catholic Church following the ordination of women in 1993). Yet some evangelicals have views not too dissimilar. They would be more likely to suggest them, however, in the context of a biblical exposition. In 1970, the *Ladies' Home Journal* was given an exegesis of Genesis 1:26–28 by a foremost evangelist. According to the author, the passage indicated that God had created a natural order for man and woman: "The biological assignment was basic and simple: Eve was to be the child-bearer, and Adam was to be the breadwinner. . . . Wife, mother, homemaker—this the appointed destiny of real womanhood."[9]

Yet, the passage contains nothing at all about breadwinning, child-bearing, or homemaking, and not a word about biology or destiny. The verses in Genesis are about something much bigger, namely, God's power in creating the human race, making male and female together in the image of God, and giving them the cultural mandate. The passage is, in fact, extraordinarily inclusive. "God blessed *them* and said to *them,* 'Be fruitful and increase in number'" (v. 28, emphasis added). Far from being a handbook on *difference,* this passage makes no differentiation between the man and the woman at all. They are allocated no different tasks or distinct roles according to some differences in nature. They both receive identical instructions and are given the blessings of God.

So where does this exegesis come from? Not from Scripture but from ideas already held in a particular cultural context about the roles of male and female. Now, this author had no ax to grind and, indeed, over the thirty years since then has shown himself to be affirming of women in ministry. Yet others do have axes to grind and have, for the last two decades, made it their mission to attack the idea of women in ministry. The development of a consumerist, American, macho culture, claiming the right to be *the* interpreters of scriptural truth, has produced an evangelicalism that is often nationalistic, right-wing, and patriarchal. The biggest disappointment is that it cannot see that its own assumptions are anything but biblical. Contributors to the debate are polarized into "camps," and any subtleties or complexities of the gender debate are quickly lost. In contemporary publications we see gender concepts still subsumed under sexual difference; we still read justifications of "essentialism" that masquerade as biblical wisdom. In an article in 1991, for example, on "rearing masculine boys and feminine girls," we are solemnly warned about the dangers of fathers "stepping into the vacuum" created by working mothers:

> In cases where the father does increase participation in child rearing, it has been suggested that the differences in the mother's and father's role in the family may become blurred as the father becomes involved in historically feminine roles. This may result in greater difficulty for children to distinguish between proper male and female roles.[10]

The comment, however, completely begs the question, What are proper male and female roles? Not only have these changed considerably over time, but the Bible is also remarkably silent about gender roles in parenting and household activities. In fact, whenever the issue comes up at all, the teaching is almost always non-differentiating. Both parents are to train up the child in the way he should go, and children are to obey *both* parents. There is no suggestion that the "proper" role of the wife is in child-rearing and domestic chores, and the "proper" role of the husband is to be exempt from them. In the letters of St. Paul, the only time the man is singled out as a father is when he is told not to be harsh with his children. Whatever the author of the above article had in mind, it was not based on Scripture but on other ideas and interpretations. The ideology of the culture is stronger than the inclusiveness of the Bible.

"Christian" Premodernism

Although this sounds exactly like the premodern position I described earlier, there is a distinction. The key factor that constitutes male-female difference for most of these writers is not just nature, or biology. It is *authority.* They believe that at the heart of male-female relationships lies a divinely decreed order of rule or sanction, the principle of "masculine headship." Some interpret this to mean that men have operative jurisdiction throughout the whole of creation. Others believe such rule is applicable only in marriage, family, and church relationships. Either way, this difference underlies all other differences between men and women. And because adherents to this position insist that this principle is laid down by God, it cancels out any other considerations that might modify or contradict it.

Take the important principle of "equal rights" for example. One author asks, "Does a wife possess under God all the rights that her husband has *in an unqualified sense?*" The answer from this author is clearly no, for the man has authority over the wife and his marriage: "The ideal of 'equal rights' in an unqualified sense is not Biblical."[11] However, this kind of thinking is poor and dangerous. If women have no "unqualified" equal rights because they are women, this denies the fundamentals of American liberty and leaves women open to "justifiable" abuse within marriage. It also betrays a confusion between the legal and the domestic. Whatever relationship might be suggested between husband and wife theologically, there is no biblical reason whatsoever for suggesting that the wife does not possess equal *rights,* which is a legal concept. The implied concession that there might be some "qualified" sense of equal rights is, of course, completely misleading. Equal rights that are qualified are not equal.

It is sad that a magnificent passage on marriage (Eph. 5:22–33) has been subject to such crass and banal interpretations. More than that, it has been used to make precisely the point Paul elsewhere ruled out. To start with, there is no reference to headship in this passage. The word in Greek is *kephale,* meaning literally "head," the complex organ at the top of the neck. Whenever it is used without its literal meaning, it is used metaphorically. There are always great dangers in building a theology on a metaphor, especially if there is any confusion about the meaning of the metaphor. Yet, most of these writers see no ambiguity at all. Ignoring the fact that Paul is using a careful literary device here, they nail the meaning down. They decide that "head" must mean "authority," construct the notion that "headship" means "male authority," and see it as a general, creational mandate. In two quick stages we have moved from a gentle metaphor to a universal principle!

The problem with this, as most reliable scholars have regularly pointed out, is that in the Greek of Paul's day, "authority" was not one of the meanings of *kephale.* And if Paul had wanted to say that men were in authority over their wives, he would certainly have said so. Elsewhere, in 1 Corinthians 7, Paul does in fact use the normal Greek word for authority *(exousia)* in describing the marriage relationship. But here, that authority is *entirely mutual and reciprocal:* Men have the authority over their wives' bodies, and wives have authority over their husbands' bodies. It is interesting how little attention is ever paid by those interested in "headship" to Paul's clear teaching in this passage. In Ephesians 5, however, Paul does *not* use the word *authority* but plays with a subtle metaphor, chosen, I believe, because it reminds us of the intense closeness of the marriage union. A head and the rest of a body cannot be separated if life is to continue. The metaphor denotes the interlocking union between husband and wife and the deep sense of love and respect that should characterize their relationship. And all of this is placed in the context of mutual submission (Eph. 5:21: "Submit to one another out of reverence for Christ").

103

Unfortunately, male authority has become such a fixation among these commentators that virtually every metaphor has to be read in this way. We apparently run into the same "biblical" problem, for example, when the men who are in authority decide to relax certain restrictions on women:

> It seems clearly contrary to the apostle's teaching, for some to argue that the male elders in the church may give a woman the right to give the exposition of the Word of God to the church and to say that, since

she does it under the authority of the male leadership, this activity would be acceptable. Paul rules out such an activity and underscores this by saying that in the public teaching situation where men are present, a woman must remain "silent" with respect to this activity and not "speak" (1 Tim. 2:12, 1 Cor. 14:34–35).[12]

This means that even if they felt inclined to be inclusive, men may not share their authority with women and listen attentively while they use their gifts of communication. They may not do this because they are men.

It is interesting, incidentally, that even though the author here is very sure about his position, he has come to it through less than rigorous scholarship. When we consult the two passages he quotes, we find he has compounded them together, even though they are about different things. The passage in Timothy does not make any reference to the "public teaching situation," and the word for "teach" or "explain" *(didasko)* is one that the New Testament itself uses with approval of a woman (Priscilla—Acts 18:26). Therefore, while there is certainly a prohibition here, it is specific to the situation and cannot be universal for all women. In 1 Corinthians 14, the context is church worship, but here the Greek word *speak* does not mean "teach" but something altogether different. Paul is asking that worship be orderly and dignified, not confused and noisy. The women, therefore, should not interrupt the worship with "chatter" (or it could mean "give ecstatic utterances") but should speak to their husbands later, at home.

The various textual interpretations are not, however, the key point. The crucial issue is what underlies the interpretations: the belief that women's nature decrees them as different from men, and thus subordinate to men, and that this insistence is sanctioned by divine *fiat*, that God has ordained it as a universal principle. Women are therefore charged to respect the roles that God has assigned for men and not try to usurp them. Anything in the New Testament that suggests some other perspective is argued away or particularized. The position rests, as before, on an unyielding essentialism. The difference is that it is now reinforced not just by biology but by theology.

A premodern perspective often seems to its followers to offer the only way of organizing relationships between women and men, and they cling to the traditionalism that embodies it as the last bastion of Christian orthodoxy. People from outside the faith have pointed out more than once that such patriarchal patterns are spread across many fundamentalist religious groups, irrespective of which religion they adhere to. Mary Daly calls patriarchy the "prevailing religion of the entire planet" with "sexual caste as a universal phenomenon."[13] Yet, we ought to be cautious, to say the least, when our theology of gender relationships is seen to have more in common with non-Christian faiths than with the faith the gospel offers. In spite of a similar ethical base, Christianity is profoundly different from the belief system embraced within Islam or ultraorthodox Judaism. It has a theology of grace.

Because the experience and self-knowledge of so many women in the church have been out of step with the dictates of premodern ideology, groups of women are actively trying to promote a Christian alternative. The work of biblical renewal and liberation has been going on for two decades now and has permeated many areas of the church. Yet, other women are less convinced that the church will ever hear them and are turning away altogether from what it has to offer. Many are exploring other options, including different expressions of the modernist and postmodern alternatives I examined earlier. The next chapter looks at the various responses of those who believe there has to be another way.

MODERN TO POSTMODERN IN THEOLOGY AND GENDER

t is difficult to say when the modernist reaction to the traditional position on male-female roles first appeared in Christianity. The Reformation itself broke new ground in thinking about church office, and in the centuries that followed, women occupied more varied roles. By the nineteenth century, certainly many Christian women writers strongly questioned traditional ideas. As they saw the injustices around them, the vision of these pioneers became a large one: Everything from suffrage to temperance was seen as part of women's Christian concerns.

However, it would be misleading to classify any of this as "modernity"; it was just an expression of good biblical sense! The modernity to which Jean Joseph Goux refers was ushered in with the start of what is now called feminist theology. In particular, Valerie Saiving Goldstein's article in 1960, "The Human Situation: A Feminine View,"[1] was pivotal. In it, she asked that those involved in religious studies, who had previously considered only male experience, open themselves to consider also distinctly female experience. It was a timely article, and by the early 1970s, a plethora of books, conferences, and women's caucuses had grown up within the churches.

HIDDEN HISTORY OF WOMEN

Some women theologians got to work, reclaiming women's hidden history in the story of Christianity. Biblical feminists had much to work with. Mary Magdalene, Joanna, Susanna, Mary, and Martha all received new attention, along with the nameless women whose stories are told in the Gospels. The women in the Acts of the apostles also came into their own: Junia the apostle, Priscilla the teacher, the four prophet-daughters of Philip, Lydia the tradeswoman, Phoebe the deacon, and all the other women listed in Paul's letters to the new Christians.

Other feminists were interested in church history and rediscovered the many women concealed from view or silenced by time: scholars, martyrs, mystics, mothers, prophets, preachers, and evangelists. They found third-century Monica, the mother of Augustine; Marcella, sister to Basil and Gregory of Nyssa and friend to John Chrysostom; and Blandina the early Christian martyr. In the convents they discovered Hildegard of Bingen, Hilda of Witby, Mother Julian of Norwich, and Teresa of Avila. When studying the Reformation they found Augusta; Margaret Fell, the Quaker leader; and women in the Tractarian movement. A century later the Ladies of the Scottish Covenant were heard again, their voices clear.

The nineteenth century particularly came alive, with women preachers and evangelists such as Phoebe Palmer; the women in the abolition movement, Lucretia Mott, the Grimke sisters (Lucy and Angelina), Antoinette Brown, Lucy Stone, Sojourner Truth (a freed slave), Harriet Tubman, and the Blackmore sisters; and women such as Elizabeth Fry, Florence Nightingale, and Josephine Butler, all active in social reform. For many of these pioneers, their involvement in the abolition movement in the United States and reform movements in Britain had drawn them to reexamine the Bible, to test whether it could really be used to justify the restrictions placed on women.[2]

While others were simply retelling the Bible stories and redoing Christian history, the modernist theologians were mounting their own attack on premodern notions of difference. Within many of the churches this was radical indeed, like "picking up the ground on which we stand and shaking it."[3] But the ground had to be shaken and a firmer base found on which to stand. Weak arguments from nature had to be exposed. Rosemary Radford Ruether spelled it out:

> To put it bluntly there is no biological connection between male gonads and the capacity to reason. Likewise there is no biological connection between female sexual organs and the capacity to be intuitive, caring or nurturing. . . . There is no necessary (biological) connection between reproductive complementarity and either psychological or social role differentiation. These are the work of culture and socialisation, not of nature.[4]

Letha Scanzoni and Nancy Hardesty took up the same theme:

> Biology is not destiny and neither hormonal nor animal studies offer proof that human gender roles are innate. Rather they are assigned and reinforced through social learning. The meaning and content of the labels "masculine" and "feminine" are totally determined by culture.[5]

All the old ideologies about a woman's place, roles, gifts, and abilities were challenged and found wanting. Instead of "difference," the focus shifted, as in equality feminism, to "similarity." Women and men had so much in common, and suddenly, the modernist perspective found a strong if unexpected echo in the traditional faith of the church. Had not Christianity always recognized that men and women share a common humanity as the image of God, a common sinfulness as rebellious creatures, a common redemption in Christ, who died for us, a common blessing in the gifts and outpouring of the Holy Spirit, and a common calling to faithfulness in the kingdom of God? To move into a united sense of being male and female, we needed to recover what had been missing so far: We needed to hear from women. The argument was unassailable. "Since being female is as much the predominant human experience as being male, the insights and experiences of women are as valuable as those of men."[6] A theology that acknowledged unity and embraced the fundamental call to freedom and equality could indeed speak Good News into the lives of women.

Yet, for all the apparent solidarity of the original vision, there were different perspectives within theological feminism from the start. Many did not have a revolutionary agenda. They simply wanted the churches to affirm greater liberty for women. They wanted men and women to read the Bible faithfully and recognize its radical message, to see gender not as a series of legalisms and restrictions on women but as the faithful response of the church to the freedom Christ brings. Exegetical analysis of dozens of key words, such as *ezer* (helpmeet), *adam* (humankind), *kephale* (head), *exousia* (authority), and *authenteo* (to have power over), as well as careful reexamination of the few problematic Pauline passages, brought new insights that did not support the restrictive position.

Other feminists, however, were more skeptical of this procedure from the start. Their theology had a more fundamental aim: to release women's experience as the *dominant* hermeneutical tool and free theology from the constraints of its sexist past. For them, the Bible was riddled with male chauvinist attitudes and had been too long in the service of patriarchy to be of any use in the liberation of women. In fact, in response to the suggestion that the Bible could be effectively "depatriarchalized," Mary Daly mused about what length such a "Bible" might be. She suggested that there might be enough salvageable material to provide an interesting pamphlet.

Feminist Theologians—A Broad Church?

Based on these differences of emphasis, and also of belief, feminist theology is now characterized by a number of different nuances and positions. By definition they are not static, for the very point of feminist theology is not to create new systems. Yet, the existence of these positions is incontrovertible. The task of feminist theology is not systematic but episodic, to allow theology to come from our midst, but the positions vary in what they see as the key task of feminist theologizing and in how they identify the Christian faith. One thing is clear, however. Nothing has been left as it was. All fundamental questions of Christian doctrine, liturgy, language, and God have been reexamined with the aim to represent the Christian faith in a way that women are able to accept for themselves.

However, women, like men, often fail to agree, and now feminist theology encompasses a wide range of opinions, beliefs, perspectives, and attitudes. Some feminist theologians are "equality theologians," looking for ways to release the common gifts of women and men. Others are liberation theologians, mystics, eco-feminists, goddess feminists, women-identified feminists, and post-Christian feminists. Even the categories "modern" and "postmodern" tend to break down as the boundaries become blurred. Some who begin with a modernist meta-narrative of equality sometimes slide into postmodern deconstruction without even noticing. Beneath all this are the questions, What can now be accepted as Christian revelation? Who speaks for God? One way to understand feminist theology is to examine this issue of revelation, for then the differences become evident.

The Bible as Canonical

When examining the question about the status of the Bible, the first option is the one that offers fewest breaks with the past. Biblical feminists accept that the Bible passed down through the centuries is canonical—God's revelation to us. Yet, they insist that it has something to say to them personally as women, not just as adjuncts to men. Culturally formed gender differences are no hindrance to God, for God searches out and speaks to women as they are.

Strictly speaking, however, biblical feminism is not part of a modernist reaction. Certainly it rejects the reductionism of premodernity and argues that culture, not biology, is key in shaping and framing our gender roles. It discards the essentialist assumptions that are often brought to the Bible and believes that Scripture supports a retelling of the story of God's relationship with women, which cuts through most of the patriarchy of the past. Biblical feminists subject the Bible to a rigorous study so they can understand its origins, culture, and the nuances evident in its human authors. They do not deny that the Bible also contains stories that can never be encouraging to women, those "texts of terror," such as the gang rape in Judges 19, which Phyllis Trible says cannot bring anything but sorrow for women. (For Trible, even these stories still have to be told, not with any hope of blessing but simply "in memoriam"[7] for those women who have been broken under patriarchy.) Biblical feminism acknowledges all these as crucial issues for women, but by doing so, it incurs the wrath of many theological traditionalists who see biblical feminism as the enemy, with little understanding of its crucial work.

At the same time, biblical feminists are at odds epistemologically with much of the rest of feminist theology, for they reject the primacy of women's experience as the interpretative framework with which to approach the Bible. For them, although experience is crucially important, it cannot be the standpoint from which we understand reality. As authentic communication from God, the biblical text cannot simply be subject to women's experience as some "higher order" that ultimately arbitrates over it. Women's experience cannot have the last word, for experience itself has to be examined and understood. There has to be an intricate two-way relationship of experience and revelation, in which experience is seen in relation to God. Since the basis of human identity is given, created by God, not simply constructed out of the particulars of our world, we have to be prepared to allow the depths of God's revelation to interpret us as we seek to understand our worth and calling before God.

If we remove biblical feminism from the modernist reaction, what is left? I suggest the work of Elisabeth Schussler Fiorenza, Judith Plaskow, Anne Carr, Elizabeth Johnson,[8] Sandra Schneiders, and the early Rosemary Radford Ruether, and I want to use two of them now as illustrations.

A Canon outside the Canon

Elisabeth Schussler Fiorenza argues that feminist theology is a critical theology, born out of women's experience of misogyny. Because much of that misogyny is related to the way in which Scripture and tradition have been used, we cannot simply identify canonical truth with the Bible as it has been traditionally received by the church. The Bible first has to be subjected to critical scrutiny and the "hermeneutics of consent" withdrawn. Then a "hermeneutics of suspicion" will help us to see what has been left out, namely, women's history, women's stories, and women's participation in the development of faith. Due to their difference from men, women have been silenced and oppressed, even by Scripture itself.

> Because of its allegiance to the defeatedness in history, a feminine crit-ical theology maintains that the hermeneutics of consent which under-stands itself as the actualising continuation of the Christian history of interpretation, does not suffice. Such a hermeneutics overlooks the fact that Christian Scripture and tradition are not only a source of truth but also of untruth, repression and domination. Since the hermeneu-tical contextual paradigm seeks only to understand the Biblical text it cannot adequately take into account the fact that the Christian past as well as its interpretation has victimised women.[9]

Old allegiances to the Bible, therefore, have to be challenged, not least the assumptions that the patriarchal texts of Scripture are in some way authoritative and an intrinsic part of the Word of God. And because the Bible cannot function as the main weapon in the political struggle for women's liberation, women need a new foundation. For Fiorenza this foundation is to be found in the *ekklesia* of women: "The her-meneutical centre of feminist biblical interpretation is the women-church *(ekklesia gynaikon)*, the movement of self-identified women and women-identified men in biblical religion."[10] This means, in effect, that Fiorenza offers us an alternative canon to that of Scripture:

113

> The locus or place of divine revelation and grace is therefore not the Bible or the tradition of a patriarchal church but the *ekklesia* of women and the lives of women who live the "option for our women selves." It is not simply "the experience" of women but the experience of women (and all those oppressed) struggling for liberation from patriarchal oppression.[11]

In this "canon outside the Canon," the real place of revelation is in the lives of women who live, and have lived, authentic lives. Their sto-ries do not have to be recorded in Scripture or in the history of the church; this is no process of merely identifying role models. Instead, through the lives of those who struggle with hardship and suffering, women find the truth of who they are. In reflecting on their refusal to accept patriarchy, women have a way of interpreting the rest of reality.

It is important to note that Fiorenza is not calling for a rejection of the Bible or of the Christian metanarrative. Rather, the Bible needs to be interpreted aright, for its message has been ambiguous: "The Bible is used against women in our liberation struggle, and perpetuates alienation from ourselves and at the same time has provided and still provides authorisation and visions for Christian women in our struggle against patriarchal racism, sexism, classism and colonialism."[12] So the Bible contains much that meets the needs of the oppressed and brings freedom and release, and this we need to hear. In this sense she is closer to the tradition of the church than many other feminist theologians, recognizing what one writer has called a "liberative core masked by centuries of misogyny."[13] Fiorenza does not want to relinquish the past completely. Where the Bible echoes the liberation that we see in the lives and confessions of those who bring the Good News, we can recognize that it is the truth of God. Where it does not, it need have no claim on our allegiance.

Although Fiorenza is part of the modernist challenge to theology, there is a paradox at the heart of her position that is outside modernity. In locating revelation in the experience of women, she seems to offer some universal concept as a hermeneutical tool. Yet, we quickly find that it is only *some* women who are the bearers of revelation, only *some* experience that we need to start from. So who makes the decision about the experience that counts? A higher authority than women's experience needs to decide what of all women's experience is the authentic core. Yet, this higher authority is denied. What is more, women's experience itself is splintering, and it has become difficult to retrieve any sort of universal base. Many different voices can be heard, and feminist theology is now accused of having a white, Western, middle-class, elitist base. African-American "womanist" theologians, Hispanic "Mujerista" theologians, and Korean Christian-shamanists all insist that their own experiences and traditions are not recognized or addressed by white feminists. Equality and similarity are the wrong concepts. Difference is crucial. In the midst of all the challenges, the door is open once again for postmodernity, and many other feminist theologians have walked through it.

A Canon within the Canon

Rosemary Radford Ruether is one of the most prolific of feminist theologians. Her concerns are varied and include church history, philosophy, language, eco-feminism, Christology, soteriology, religious experience, and comparative religion. She has written a great deal and her position has gone through a number of stages, both of which make her work difficult to summarize. At one level she shares the modernist commitment to equality, claiming that the "egalitarian, counter-cultural vision is the true norm of Christianity." She also never quite leaves behind a version of essentialism or foundationalism, although sometimes what she sees as her foundation is unclear:[14] "I would see Scripture as normative, not in the sense of infallible truths disclosed from beyond normal experience, or as unique experiences incomparable with other experiences, but rather as a foundational memory."[15]

Ruether has often been linked with Fiorenza, although the two have very different interests and styles of writing. Like Fiorenza, Ruether begins with a basic belief in the retainability of the Christian tradition, while seeing the need to rid it of its androcentricity. Yet, unlike Fiorenza, Ruether did not initially look outside the Bible for an alternative locus of revelation in the liberation-experience of the community of women. She did not want to produce a dichotomy between tradition and experience. For her, that was not necessary. What after all are Scripture and tradition other than "codified, collective human experience"? And what is experience other than "experience of the divine, experience of oneself, and experience of the community and the world"?[16] The Scriptures are the "past experiences" of the community of believers, and the task for the contemporary believing community is to appropriate "the foundational paradigm as the continuing story of its own redemption in relation to God."[17] She recognizes, however, that this is difficult, because "revelation is said to be closed and located in the past." The faith has been codified and locked in so that the "ongoing power of the Spirit sent by Christ to the community is no longer able to 'blow where it will' but is institutionalised in the authority of bishops."[18] God's real revelation, therefore, must be released from Scripture and the church to live again, and the "authority of the official canonical framework [must be] overturned" so that the egalitarian vision can be realized.

Ruether, therefore, formulates her "canon within the Canon." She takes the prophetic-messianic principle from Scripture and makes that her benchmark for true biblical faith. The call of the prophets away from injustice and idolatry, the bias to the poor and marginalized, the servant-leadership of Jesus of Nazareth all fit with her understanding of the redemptive kernel of the Christian message. The new essentialism is not tradition, biology, or Scripture but justice for women. Therefore, the new hermeneutical principle is that "whatever denies, diminishes and distorts the full humanity of women is, therefore, appraised as not redemptive."[19]

With this new interpretative framework, the entire biblical message is transformed, becoming itself a critique of injustice, oppression, and patriarchy. Much of what has been accepted as legitimate practice in church history and contemporary Christianity is now outside the boundaries of a redemptive biblical hermeneutic. What is more, those texts of Scripture that were used to justify the practices can also be relegated to the rubbish bin. Only what is fully redemptive may remain.

One issue has been at the center of most of the concerns of those Christians who have not been won over by the modernist critique: the place of Christ. If, as Ruether insists, revelation is not fixed or static but in a process of constant revision and response, where does that leave the notion that Christ is the unique revelation of God? And where does it place the death of Christ as the redemptive act for the sins of the world?

Ruether tackles this in a number of writings. She sees the messianic principle demonstrated in the way Jesus takes on not kingship and domination but humility. Jesus "drastically reverses the social references of divine redemptive activity." But to talk of Jesus as the *unique* representation of God would be misleading. It would also lead us back into all the problems of maleness that have so dogged the premodern tradition. "Christ as redemptive person and Word of God, is not to be encapsulated 'once for all' in the historical Jesus" but in the community of liberation today.

> This kind of Spirit Christology does not separate out a past perfect historical Jesus from the ongoing Spirit. Rather it sees Christ as a power that continues to be revealed in persons, both male and female, in the

present. Christ is located in a new humanity that discloses the future potential of redeemed life. The reality of Christ is not completed in the past but continues to be disclosed in the present.[20]

The historical Christ and the redeeming Christ, therefore, are no longer the same. The historical Christ was a man. The redeeming Christ is an ongoing messianic-liberating principle, revealed in a new humanity in which issues of gender difference or male-female distinctions are no longer relevant.

Many questions remain about the method and direction of Ruether's work. In her later writings she seems to give women's experience a greater status as an interpretative tool. Two related questions come to mind when trying to understand where Ruether is now. The first is whether she can justifiably be called a theist. Daphne Hampson thinks not: "It seems to me questionable that Ruether herself is theistic. . . . In fact, if one reads her work carefully, one notices that she never speaks of God, but rather of people's concept of God, which may lead them on in their striving for justice."[21]

The second question is whether Ruether is on an inevitable journey into the relativism of postmodernity and, indeed, is so far down the road that it no longer matters to her whether any metanarrative is true or not. She may well be, for if women's experience is ultimately all we need to deconstruct reality, what we reconstruct in its place is a matter of personal preference not belief.

POSTMODERNITY IN THEOLOGY AND GENDER

Most postmodern feminists are no longer engaged in feminist theology from within the church. The key players have left. Yet, ironically, they walked out as modernists, rather than as a postmodern gesture. Mary Daly left Christianity more than twenty-five years ago, claiming,

We cannot really belong to institutional religion as it exists. It isn't good enough to be token preachers. It isn't good enough to have our energies drained and co-opted. Singing sexist hymns, praying to a male god breaks our spirit, makes us less than human. The crushing weight of this tradition, of this power structure tells us that *we do not even exist.*[22]

Daphne Hampson similarly shook the dust off her feet, arguing that she could not assent to the fundamental belief system of the Christian faith. She recognized that Christianity is based on the beliefs that there is a reality beyond our experience and the author of that reality is God. For her, a commitment to Christianity entails an acceptance of this metanarrative. Yet, she believes it is untrue and that its untruth can be seen in its practices. She rejects Christianity's beliefs and therefore is not a Christian.

A departure from the Christian faith was for each of them a matter of integrity. They did not agree with its foundation or its practices, so they felt they had to go. These reactions were themselves in keeping with modernity. The appeal was still to a framework of truth: the stand was for one metanarrative over another.

It was not until she was well out of the Christian faith that Mary Daly's work took on the distinct postmodern nuance it has today. Yet, what is interesting now is that postmodern unbelievers do not usually leave the church, whether they are men or women, especially if they are receiving a salary. Why should they? If there are no metanarratives anyway, then it matters little whether one stays or goes. One is free to choose one's own style and option. Since not only gender but also God is a linguistic construct (reinforced by practices and rituals), we are free to construct or deconstruct when and where we will. Belief is simply choice of style or preference.

Postmodern feminist theology does more than focus on difference. It uses difference in its deconstruction of "god." One earlier route was through the "emancipation" of the goddess. Many argued that the goddess has always been there, hidden from view in most of the world's institutional religions and overlaid by centuries of male thinking. That is why throughout the history of religion she has frequently "appeared" in various forms and guises. In Catholicism, for example, she comes in the form of the Virgin, and in building statues and shrines to Mary and receiving miracles from the hand of Mary, we are implicitly recognizing her divinity. But beneath this Virgin Mother, who has been captured and domesticated by the Catholic Church, is none other than the embodiment of the fundamental religious female principle that undergirds the whole of reality. The premoderns were right to fear women because the female principle is a powerful, cosmic force, which, once freed, heralds a new era for women.

Others argue in a similar way for the "Christa," the female representation of Christ, who more truly than the man epitomizes the sacrifice that is made for the sins of the world, for women have suffered the sins of sexism, male violence, and oppression. They have indeed given their bodies to be broken. Others argue for "Sophia," the wisdom of God as the divine, eternal, feminine principle. Christianity unfolds the cloths that have hidden God in feminine form, and she is released as the Spirit of wisdom and truth.

These postmodernists were interested in the goddess as a reversal of the "male God" present in Christianity through the ages, for God of Christian tradition is *fundamentally* male, not only in name but in all his attributes. Daphne Hampson sees this "God" as a projection of the Western male psyche, and he therefore incorporates all the characteristics of power, supremacy, authority, divine-rightness, and self-sufficiency prized by men. She described the reaction of one of her students on recognizing that the Christian understanding of God incorporated what she disliked most in human beings: "Now I understand why I have no use for such a god." For some feminists the way forward was to rediscover the god(dess) as the one who gives our experiences meaning.

Most postmodern writers, however, resist the "reification" of the goddess. To embrace difference does not mean to replace the male "God-Father" with the female "Goddess-Mother." It means deconstructing God altogether. Consequently, in *Beyond God the Father,* Mary Daly not only rejects the idea that women need some "male divinity and his son" to save them, she also discards "God" as the name of any deity, personal or impersonal. It makes little actual difference whether this God has feminine gender, inclusive gender, or no gender, for the process of deconstruction is not complete until we realize that "God" is not a noun at all. God is a verb: active, dynamic, moving. God is not a being, but be-ing, the "I am" of women coming into their own authentic liberation. In the "original reintroduction" to Daly's volume, written for the second edition ten years later, she

119

attempts to explain the consequences of not sufficiently deconstructing God:

> Naming Be-ing as Verb is an essential leap in the cognitive/affective
> journey beyond patriarchal fixations. Serious and unacknowledged dif-
> ficulties can arise when those who speak and/or write of the Goddess
> of goddesses avoid the giant step/leap of Realising ultimate/intimate
> reality as movement, as Verb. One result, though unintended is com-
> plicity in Verbicide—killing of the living, transforming energy of
> words, muting of the metamorphic, shape-shifting power inherent in
> words. Thus, the Goddess can be reduced to a static symbol, a mere
> replacement for the noun God.[23]

It is only in participation with the Verb that women can be "saved,"
and the salvation they need is salvation from sexism, for women are
the innocents. Salvation is liberation, freedom to be powerful and
released so that "raging/Racing women become Counterclock-Wise,
asking Counterclock-Whys. Boundary-shifting Sibyls become Other-
Wise, uttering Other Whys. Our very being vibrates with earth, air,
fire, water, and with the moon, sun and farthest stars."[24]

In both her concepts and presentation, Daly aims to go beyond the
bounds of patriarchal religion, deconstructing every aspect of the language in which this religion is expressed. The goal is a dynamic
exchange in which all that has been influenced by male thought forms,
including, most particularly, words themselves, are redone—reem-
ployed in a new representation of woman. Perhaps not surprisingly,
however, this is regarded by some as obscurantist, smacking again of
the elitism and self-indulgence that they see as characteristic of much
postmodern feminism. She faces the accusation, as does Luce Irigaray,
of being out of touch and uninterested in women's real battles, especially in non-white, post-colonial cultures. Her later books continue
to attempt this perpetual redoing of our language, beyond patriarchy.

Daly is long gone from the church, but Carter Heyward is still in
it. Yet, her deconstruction of "god," and her use of god-as-verb is no
less radical than Daly's. She images Christa, not as reified goddess but
as the spirit and process in a woman's lovemaking. In a curious reversal of the premodern position, she echoes the idea that women have

a different spiritual identity, closely tied to their sexuality. Yet, that difference is not for men to define. Women must claim it for themselves in lesbian sexuality. God becomes the verb "to god," and it is in "godding," especially in "sexual godding," that women experience their authentic identity most fully. In one passage she describes a passionate lovemaking between women in terms that evoke and fuse it with the Eucharist:

> There is no greater delight than to celebrate and share the body of Christa as eternal resource of nourishment on the sacred journey towards justice. I praise her as both ground and figure of our lovemaking. She is in the power between us, in our relation as well as in the persons we are and are becoming, you and I together. I see her in you and I enjoy her in myself. I take her and stroke her playfully. I look upon her with immense tenderness. I take her and nibble a little, I take her and eat, take her and drink. I am taken, grasped, and caressed by her power moving between us. Immersing myself in you, with you, through you, I move with you in the sensual wellspring of her love. I move with you in the turbulence of her passion.[25]

Not only are our gender and sexuality constructed, to be reconstructed along lines of "openness" and "love," god can similarly be reconstructed. In this passage, god is the dynamic process through which this openness takes place. Heyward (like Daly) seems to feel that this process can still deliver a basis for ethics. But what kind of ethics, and how does it engage with other people? The problem is that no critique or ethical direction she offers can be binding on others, for others' experience might be different, and their processes of deconstruction might have quite a different shape. At most, postmodern feminist theology can only assemble pastiches of ideas, morality, and meanings. Beyond that there is little to be said.

PARALLELS WITH SECULAR FEMINISM

Feminist theology is more than a reaction against the essentialism of a premodern attitude. It is also a reaction against the abuses of a religion that has sometimes used its authority to deny both full human-

121

ity and dignity to women. In that sense its origins in the Second Wave are similar to the origins of secular feminism. Its concerns for a new interpretation of the structures of our lives committed to equality and justice also parallel the concerns of modernist feminists in all other spheres. Similarly, postmodern feminist theology parallels many of the moves made by other postmodern feminists, with an identical interest in deconstruction and experience-based analyses of reality.

Yet, in far more ways, feminist theology is different from secular feminism. In asking the same implicit questions about the nature of reality, sexuality, gender, and human personhood, it has still done so, initially at least, from within the Christian faith system. The responses that it produces are diverse because the underlying beliefs shift and diverge, but there is no "slippery slope." There is no truth in the accusation that when we start with the biblical examination of Catherine Kroeger or Gretchen Gabelein Hull,[26] we end up with the relativism of Mary Daly. The two are in different conceptual worlds, and ultimately at the heart of the difference is the growing contrast between faith and unbelief.

Post-Postmodern Postscript

The question of the origin and meaning of human sexuality is obviously important, but what we take as our starting point for the answer is vital. In trying to work through one key question in the sex and gender debate, I have had to cover much terrain. Using Jean Joseph Goux's categories of premodern, modern, and postmodern has helped me to give some shape to the inquiry and to look at different starting points. I now want to present some responses from a Christian perspective.

Premodern, Modern, and Postmodern Revisited

Each of the positions examined in this book incorporates some important insights while leaving itself open to considerable weaknesses. Premodernity acknowledges the givenness of reality, including human reality. It claims that there is something within us and beyond us that structures how we live, something that others, Jean Paul Sartre, for example, vehemently denied: "There is no human nature, since there is no God to conceive it."[1] It also believes there is truth and that we live in a universe in which, if some things are true, then their opposites are false. In its Christian form it acknowledges that the world is far bigger than human experience, and human life is to be lived before the God who is there. Some Christians have argued, too, that a premodern perspective can provide some useful tools, especially if an essentialist identity can be seen as a "representative metaphor entailing human agency and practice, rather than a realist retreat into a nature against which human beings are powerless."[2]

But this position also contains some fundamental weaknesses. Without the qualification above, premodernity has a reductionist mentality: It takes one thing in creation and absolutizes it, whether that key thing is biology, maleness, reason, or authority. Once anything is made absolute (i.e., becomes essentialist), then the rest of reality is interpreted from that standpoint, with inevitable results. Reality is distorted, the richness and variety of creation is shrunk, and the facts are now represented to fit the assumptions. What is more, we have a limited basis for our ethics, especially our gender ethics. If we begin with some "natural" evolutionary framework because it suits our assumptions, we have to recognize that the only shape to our relationships is determined ultimately by instinct and drive. But we are much more complex creatures than that. We have emotions, longings, fears, hopes, and ambitions, all of which are related to our family attitudes, our moral ideas, and our belief system. Furthermore, if we begin with an authoritarian idea of "male headship," then women's moral responses are ultimately reduced to whether they are obedient or disobedient to male structures. Yet, when we take biblical revelation seriously, the perspective we hold suggests we are all equally purposeful, responsible beings who have choice before God about the way we act.

The modernist perspective also incorporates vital insights. The attack on reductionism, especially biological reductionism, opens up reality and leaves space for the important interplay between nature and culture. This gives us a much stronger basis for ethics, for it recognizes we are moral human beings with ethical choices. It also makes it possible for us to develop concepts of justice, injustice, equality, and responsibility for our actions and for other people. However, modernity has its own grave weaknesses. It incorporates a basic separation of knowledge and faith, failing to see that knowledge itself is the outworking of faith commitments. In trying to establish a basis for knowing on the primacy of women's experience, modernist feminism (and especially feminist theology) fails to recognize that it is making a faith commitment, for underlying its own position is a view of the person as autonomous and a view of knowledge as ultimately subjective. Ultimately, modernity has irreversible internal weaknesses, for it "relies on precisely that mode of thought that is responsible for the situation it wishes to change."[3]

Finally, postmodernity incorporates an important critique of modernity. It lays bare the assumptions in modernity's position and looks at the arbitrariness of its definitions, when there is no basis from which to make them. Its questions, though cynical, need to be asked. What is "justice" other than a situation in which rich people can hire expensive lawyers to get them acquitted of crimes everyone knows they have committed? And is "gender equality" anything other than a widening of the goal posts so that women can score some of the goals usually scored by men? When the game, its rules, and its ethos have already been set within a male-designed framework, what space is left for any real involvement of women? Postmodernity also raises key issues about difference in its refutation of androgyny and in its identification of the important multiple ways our identities are shaped and formed. It pushes the "gender construction" argument to its logical conclusion, to a point at which there are no demarcations between what is structured and what is not.

But the weaknesses of postmodernity are centered inevitably on its relativism, for we are compelled to ask, Where do we deconstruct *from?* What is our starting point? Since postmodernity has no foundational starting point, it always has to deconstruct from a position of deconstruction. And when constructs are relativized, it is from a position of relativism. But this leaves a large internal problem with the very formulation of a postmodern position. What does it mean to say, "Everything is relative"? If the statement itself has merely a relative status, it cannot be in any sense binding, for it is not making any claim to truth. But if "everything is relative" has an absolute status and claims truth

125

for itself, then it negates its own formulation. Yet, though the claim to relativism cannot be articulated, it still tries to be prescriptive. It continues to insist that nothing is fixed, and we may not make categorical statements. In fact, relativism is at best an absolutization of indifference.

The categories of premodern, modern, and postmodern have not given us fine details or delineation, but they have given us the shape of the landscape, drawn out the patterns and clusters for us to observe. In trying to make my own response, I could argue that a Christian perspective in some ways incorporates elements of all three positions, and this would be a reasonable observation. Elaine Graham, in her chapter on a way forward, outlines a call for a "constructed essentialism, one which has recourse to a notion of fixed coherent identity, but only as a strategic and enacted category."[4] This would be an interesting program to develop, but I could also say that the time has come for me to leave these categories behind. They have done a useful job, but they have their limitations. They are adequate for a rough sketch but far too vague and nebulous if we are trying to copy a masterpiece.

SOME CHRISTIAN RESPONSES

As an alternative strategy, I want to start by offering another Archimedean point (which, as we saw earlier, is a place from which we can survey reality or get an outlook on the world). A perspective that attempts to remain faithful to the historic Christian faith begins from a different location from that of biology, or of culture, or of experience. It starts from the acceptance that God exists as does a world of which we are part. And although this might sound very different from all the other starting points we have examined, the assumptions it makes are not of a fundamentally different order. The assumption that human beings construct reality out of their own minds and experiences or that all of reality can be reduced to biology are both positions that rest on faith and assumptions. Indeed, all knowledge ultimately builds from a basis that is taken on trust at its most fundamental level. It is no more sweeping, therefore, to posit the existence of God than it is the belief in equality, truth, or infinite deconstruction.

The God who I am claiming is there is the God whom the Christian Scriptures, in an unfolding revelation, reveal to us. This God is a God who is relational, a God whose name is love, a God who is interpersonal and involved with the creation. This creating God is one who sets boundaries and breathes morality into the creation and who constantly offers us the opportunity to change our lives for the better. What is more, God is expressed uniquely and personally in Jesus Christ, to whom the Scriptures and the church bear witness. Christ, in union with the whole Godhead, is the one who has given his life for ours, who offers the power of the Spirit to those who ask, who shows a new kind of authority and breaks down barriers between people. Our "creedal" starting point also involves a commitment to the Bible, not simply for its narrative history or theological teachings but because it discloses who God is and who we are and unlocks the truth of God for us. But the Bible has to be understood correctly, which means we must also recognize that we might get it wrong. Our experience is not the primary exegetical hermeneutic. Rather, the Bible contains its own hermeneutical tools: It holds the truth to its own meaning and interpretation.

From this perspective, many things follow. To begin with, we can accept that our sexuality is indeed a given, part of the deep created structure of our humanness. The differences in our sexual makeup are part of the rich complementarity that God has breathed into creation. Yet, a creational perspective is different from a "natural" one; sexuality is not simply that which defines our "nature." Creation is ordered, not by something people used to call the laws of nature but by complex normative structures that define and delineate our various relationships. For example, we are not to murder or commit adultery; we are to love our neighbors as ourselves; we are not to steal or violate one another. God has created a norm for the structure of reality and breathed an ethical order into it, and that has implications for our sexuality. Far from being driven by the unremitting desire to procreate, we have the responsibility to use our sexuality responsibly and to act always in love. How we express our sexuality matters, and we remain accountable to God.

This is all relevant in our contemporary context. We live in a culture that is highly sexualized and suggests that because we are sexual people,

127

sexual activity is essential for us to be fully actualized, content human beings. Therefore, the idea that there are boundaries around our sexuality is not a popular one. Yet, premodernity, modernity, or postmodernity have not given us adequate ways of thinking through what it means to be sexual beings, for to be sexual means neither that we are driven to procreate, nor that we have autonomous, unfettered choice to create our own sexual nuances or express our sexual preferences. It means that our sexuality is the dimension through which we experience our lives. And what is important from a Christian perspective is that we find appropriate sexual expressions for the relationships within which we live. Sexuality in friendship is different from that in marriage, or family relationships, or neighborhoods, or fellowship. When we confuse the integrity of each relationship, we lose something crucial.

The distinction between sex and gender is also important, because it helps us avoid the temptation to reduce everything to sex. Yet, I think it would be a mistake to think too rigidly of sex as creational and gender as cultural. This suggests too great a dichotomy—that we accept our sex as a creation of God, but we create our gender for ourselves, according to social variants. In fact, if we believe in a God who has created a normative structure for relationships, we have to believe in a God who is as interested in our gender as in our biology, for the way we shape our gender is also part of our human response before God. Therefore, we need to address issues of power, discrimination, poor communication, injustice, unfaithfulness, violation, competitiveness, and stereotypes, because in all of these areas we can contravene the principles that God has given us for gender relationships. We need to develop loving, just, impartial, faithful, and open ways of relating with one another, because then we are responding together to the God who is love, justice, righteousness, faithfulness, and truth. God calls us into responsible and right relationships, and gender patterns call from us a response of obedience.

We need, therefore, to resist crippling stereotypes whether they are racial or gender or whatever else. And we also need to recognize that despite popular exhortations, the Bible does not say a great deal about being masculine for God or feminine for Jesus! So many of the stereotypes that proliferate in "Christian" literature are far from biblical. In fact, the New Testament does not tell us how to be feminine or mascu-

128

line at all. It offers us one set of characteristics as a guideline for both sexes, the fruit of the Spirit: love, joy, peace, patience, kindness, goodness, faithfulness, gentleness, and self-control. The fact that these are often interpreted as "feminine characteristics" ought to set us thinking.

Four Paradigms

When we ask the question, How is the relationship between male and female to be understood? we do not find one (essentialist) answer in the Bible. The Bible offers a diverse response and does not focus exclusively on any single resolution, whether that be in terms of our biological differences, our gender demarcations, our different experiences, or our androgyny. In fact, woven as it is through the many different kinds of biblical literature, a biblical narrative or analysis of male-female relations is very complex. When we study the text, it is possible to detect four different underlying paradigms, which are used interchangeably to describe the relationship between men and women.

The first of these is *difference*. Perhaps that should no longer surprise us. In the Genesis story of creation, as well as in many of the narratives about sin, the idea of difference is regularly rehearsed. Eve is not the same as Adam. She is *isha* to his *ish*. Man and woman are different in terms of procreation. They also first faced temptation in different ways. She gave in when she was alone; he gave in when he was in the company of his wife. They received different penalties as a result of the fall—the woman in childbearing and the man in husbandry. Throughout Scripture woman and man are described differently. Women are the "weaker sex," says Peter, as indeed they were under the restrictions of a patriarchal society. They have different spheres of influence (although these change, as the eulogy to the woman in Proverbs 31 reminds us). The women and men surrounding Jesus had different gender roles (the women, for example, were the ones who came to anoint his body). Paul suggests different dress codes for men and women at worship, and he restrains women in some churches from exercising certain forms of leadership.

Yet, difference does not exhaust the biblical perspective. The Bible also incorporates the idea of *sameness,* or *similarity,* when looking at

129

the relationship between women and men. Again in the creation story, when the first man awoke from his sleep and saw the first woman, his cry was one of recognition, of sameness: "Here at last is bone of my bone, flesh of my flesh." At this level the Bible recognizes an element of androgyny in male-female relations. Women and men are both equal parts of the human race. They are more like each other than they are like anything else in creation. They are given the same commands to be fruitful and multiply, to replenish the earth. They are given the same status over the rest of creation, the same responsibility for procreation. They are given the same moral requirements, the same mandate against idolatry, the same requirement for faithfulness to God. In their marital sexuality, they are to have the same freedoms and constraints. In parenting, too, male and female are on a par. Children are given the same command with regard to both mother and father: They are to respect and obey each of them. What is more, within the church, women and men have the same gifting. The prophet Joel foresaw the time when God would pour out his spirit on all flesh, when sons and daughters would prophesy (Joel 2:28). And in the New Testament church the gifts were given generously and indiscriminately to believers irrespective of gender. Most of all, Paul reminds us that in Christ the dividing concepts of "male" and "female" are no longer appropriate (Gal. 3:28). In Christ we are all one. And after death, when marriage no longer exists, it seems that it is our identity and similarity to each other that goes with us into the next world.

130

The third category is *complementarity*. Women and men are not simply the same or different from each other; they are also complementary. They "fit" together; they each reciprocate and fulfill something in the other. The first man was not complemented by any of the animals he had named. They were fundamentally different from him. In one of his letters to the church at Corinth, Paul talks about the complementary nature of woman and man. In Christ woman is not independent of man, nor is man independent of woman. And just as woman came from man, now man comes from woman (1 Cor. 11:11). Correlation, reciprocity, symmetry are all built into the way male and female echo each other. Complementarity does not imply hierarchy, therefore, as many have taken it to imply. It is premised on the reciprocation and completion of female by male, and male by female.

Finally, the Bible also indicates the importance of *union*. Women and men are together the image of God. The story of the creation of man and woman stresses their "ontological union" more than anything else. The man was made as distinct from the animals, from the "dust of the earth" as a separate creation. But when Genesis tells the story of the woman's creation, God did not return to the clay to remodel a second being. Instead, out of the form of the first human, there were now two. Women and men are not ontologically different, with different spiritual identities, but they are in union as humankind. This union is followed throughout Scripture. There is a union of disobedience, a union of redemption. Both the author of Genesis and St. Paul offer us a picture of union of male and female in marriage, where they are once again "one flesh." Paul tells us that husband and wife no longer even have ownership of their own bodies. The husband has "authority" over his wife's sexuality; the wife has "authority" over her husband's. This is not to encourage possessiveness or abuse but rather so that we can know something about the union of love within our humanness. Metaphors for our unity abound in the New Testament: We are together the "body" of Christ as the church, we are together the "bride" of Christ. We are the "living stones," the "royal priesthood" together. Our deepest experiences, both physical and spiritual, are not of autonomy, difference, or separateness, but of the unity of male and female in God.

When we fail to grasp that the Bible contains each of these themes, we inevitably distort the full biblical message. In turn, that distorts our theology and leads to vehement reactions and repudiations. If we focus on only one, say difference or complementarity, as the biblical perspective, then we distort the male-female relationship and inevitably end up with hierarchy and subordination. If we focus on another, for example, sameness, we again distort the full biblical picture and reinforce androgyny and lose the significance of our differences. But when we work with all four, then we see the sweep of the biblical revelation and the space and scope it gives us to develop our relationships faithfully and creatively.

The Gospel as Deconstructive

That is why we do not need to be afraid of deconstruction, once we have the basis from which to do it. The biblical revelation actually offers a foundation from which we may contextualize the gender relationships that have developed in our societies and understand them better. The New Testament shows us how Jesus himself contextualized gender relations, sometimes stripping away centuries of patriarchal distortions. Take the Samaritan woman at the well of Sychar (John 4). The construction of race and gender in that society meant that communication between Jesus and the woman was taboo. His request for a drink of water especially transgressed the sexual, gender, race, and religious codes that he, as a Jewish male, was required to observe. He also took part in a conversation in which meanings were contested and in which he made his point powerfully through ambiguity and allusion. As a result of that conversation, the woman calls her neighbors and becomes the first evangelist.

In another story—the account of the woman with menstrual problems (Luke 8:43–48)—we see another example of how Jesus relativized gender constructions, in this case, constructions of what was clean or unclean, acceptable or unacceptable behavior for a woman. In this incident, after Jesus' clothing was touched by a menstruating woman, the "normal" response would have been for him to rebuke her for having contaminated him, making him ritually unclean, and to leave the crowd so he could go through the required ablutions. Instead, he stayed where he was, brought healing to the woman, and reinterpreted what she had done. He commended her faith and initiative, telling her to go in peace. Similar "deconstructions" of the meaning given to women are recorded in the stories of Mary and Martha, the Cyro-Phoenician woman, the widow who gave her mite for an offering, and the woman who anointed Jesus.

The fundamental questions are, From what basis should we try to understand what it means to be a human male or female, and how should we express those differences in our relationships? My argument in this final chapter is that we cannot start from within a premodern, modern, or postmodern position. The problem is that the Bible has been dismissed from most scholarship since the Enlightenment, and that dismissal has robbed our culture of a powerful basis for grasping the meaning of human personhood. When we once more take seriously the rich sweep of biblical literature, we are confronted with key themes that have traveled throughout the centuries and today help us to make sense of our relationships with each other. The narratives of creation, sin, and redemption offer us an alternative journey to that which our culture has been making. They give us a cogent framework for putting together the story of our humanness and our identity. Sexuality and gender are a crucial part of that story, as we see the damage that has been done to women and men alike and the distortions that still pervert our relationships and societal structures. But we do not see things aright by elevating our own autonomous experience, or by walking down a dead-end road to relativism. The uniqueness of the biblical alternative is that the answer to the brokenness of the past, or present, does not lie ultimately with us at all. It is in the gospel of Christ that all things can be made new.

NOTES

CHAPTER 1

1. R. M. Fagley, "The Atomic Bomb and the Crisis of Man," *Christianity and Crisis* (1 October 1945): 5.

2. In the film *The Life and Times of Rosie the Riveter* (Emeryville, Calif.: Clarity Educational Productions, 1982).

3. See, for example, Margaret Forster, *Significant Sisters: The Grass Roots of Active Feminism 1839–1939* (Harmondsworth: Penguin, 1984); H. Heney, *Australia's Founding Mothers* (Sydney: Nelson, 1978); J. A. Hone, "The Movement for the Higher Education of Women in Victoria in the Later Nineteenth Century" (master's thesis, Monash, 1966). One exception is a biography of the pioneering Australian woman Caroline Chisholm: M. Kiddle, *Caroline Chisholm* (Melbourne: Melbourne University Press, 1950).

4. Janet West, *Daughters of Freedom: A History of Women in the Australian Church* (Sutherland, Australia: Albatross Books, 1997), 22. In the same book, see also her comment on the emigrant clergy daughter Rachel Henning (23).

5. Catherine Clinton, *The Other Civil War: American Women in the Nineteenth Century* (New York: Hill and Wang, 1993), 123–31.

6. C. S. Bremer, "Appendix A: Women in the British Universities," in Mrs. Henry Sidwick, *The Place of University Education in the Life of Women* (London: Transactions of the Women's Insitute, 1897), 34–52. See also Martha Vicinus, *Independent Women: Work and Community for Single Women 1850–1920* (London: Virago History, 1985), 121–62.

7. West, *Daughters of Freedom,* 31.

8. See the work of Valerie Griffiths, especially "Women in Mission," in *Men, Women, and God,* ed. Kathy Keay (London: Marshall Pickering, 1986), 61–77.

9. West, *Daughters of Freedom,* 50–53.

10. Michel Foucault and Jean Joseph Goux, "Irigaray vs the Utopia of the Neutral Sex," in *Engaging with Irigaray,* ed. Carolyn Burke, Naomi Schor, and Margaret Whitford (New York: Columbia University Press, 1994), 189.

CHAPTER 2

1. Michel Foucault and Jean Joseph Goux, "Irigaray vs the Utopia of the Neutral Sex," in *Engaging with Irigaray,* ed. Carolyn Burke, Naomi Schor, and Margaret Whitford (New York: Columbia University Press, 1994), 189.

2. Fénelon, *Essai philosophique sur le gouvernement civil* (1921); quoted in ibid., 178.

3. *Social Trends 28,* London, Government Statistical Service, 1998.

4. Quoted in Roger Hurding, "Restoring the Image," in *Men, Women and God,* ed. Kathy Keay (London: Marshall Pickering, 1986), 293.

5. See a fuller discussion in Mary Stewart Van Leeuwen, *Gender and Grace* (Leicester: Inter-Varsity Press, 1990).

6. Anne and Bill Moir, *Why Men Don't Iron: The Real Science of Gender Studies* (London: HarperCollins, 1998), 118.

7. Ibid.

8. Richard Dawkins, *The Selfish Gene* (Oxford: Oxford University Press, 1976).

9. Quoted in Van Leeuwen, *Gender and Grace,* 104.

CHAPTER 3

1. See Michel Foucault and Jean Joseph Goux, "Irigaray vs the Utopia of the Neutral Sex," in *Engaging with Irigaray,* ed. Carolyn Burke, Naomi Schor, and Margaret Whitford (New York: Columbia University Press, 1994), 189.

2. See Shulamith Firestone, *The Dialectic of Sex: The Case for a Feminist Revolution* (London: Jonathon Cape, 1971).

3. See the report of the *New Scientist* debate in "Male Pregnancy 'Achievable Soon,'" *The Times,* London, 24 May 1984.

4. Elaine Graham, *Making the Difference: Gender, Personhood, and Theology* (London: Mowbray, 1995), 94.

5. Marian Lowe, "Sociobiology and Sex Differences," *Signs: Journal of Women in Culture and Society* 4 (1978): 55. See also Marian Lowe, "The Dialectic of Biology and Culture," in *Women's Nature: Rationalizations of Inequality,* ed. Marian Lowe and Ruth Hubbard (Oxford: Pergamon Press, 1983), 55.

6. Germaine Greer, *The Whole Woman* (London: Doubleday, 1999), 288.

7. See Trevor Stammers, *When Love Lies Bleeding* (London: Hodder & Stoughton, 1996). See also James Alsdurf and Phyllis Alsdurf, *Battered into Submission* (Downers Grove, Ill.: InterVarsity Press, 1989); Carol J. Adam, *Woman Battering* (Minneapolis: Fortress, 1994); Nancy Nason-Clark, *The Battered Wife: How Christians Confront Family Violence* (Louisville: John Knox Press, 1997).

8. Penny Summerfield, *Reconstructing Women's Wartime Lives* (Manchester: Manchester University Press, 1998), 1–42.

9. Kate Fillion, *Lip Service: The Myth of Female Virtue in Love, Sex, and Friendship* (Sydney: HarperCollins, 1996), 11.

10. Ann Oakley, *Woman's Work: The Housewife, Past and Present* (New York: Pantheon, 1974). See also Ann Oakley, *Becoming a Mother* (Oxford: Martin Robertson, 1979).

11. Oakley, *Housewife,* 100.

12. Hannah Gavron, *The Captive Wife* (London: Routledge and Kegan Paul, 1966).

13. Greer, *The Whole Woman,* 307.

14. G. Rubin, "The Traffic in Women: Notes on the 'Political Economy' of Sex," in *Toward an Anthropology of Women,* ed. R. R. Reitr (New York: Monthly Review Press, 1975), 179–80.

15. Greer, *The Whole Woman,* 308.

16. Elaine Storkey, *What's Right with Feminism* (London: SPCK, 1985). Part 2 offers an analysis of this classification.

17. Fillion, *Lip Service,* 198–261.

18. Natasha Walter, *The New Feminism* (London: Little Brown, 1998). See also Elaine Storkey, "The Same Old Story?" *Third Way* 21, no. 6 (July/August 1998): 12–14.

19. Katherine Viner, "The Personal Is Still Political," in *On the Move: Feminism for a New Generation,* ed. Natasha Walter (London: Virago, 1999), 24.

20. Greer, *The Whole Woman,* 86.

21. Ruth Hubbard, "The Emperor Doesn't Wear Any Clothes: The Impact of Feminism on Biology," in *Men's Studies Modified,* ed. Dale Spender (Oxford: Pergamon Press, 1981), 217.

22. Graham, *Making the Difference,* 170.

CHAPTER 4

1. Luce Irigaray, *J'aime a toi: Esquisse d'une felicite dans l'histoire* (Paris: Grasset, 1992), 72.

2. Michel Foucault and Jean Joseph Goux, "Irigaray vs the Utopia of the Neutral Sex," in *Engaging with Irigaray,* ed. Carolyn Burke, Naomi Schor, and Margaret Whitford (New York: Columbia University Press, 1994), 180.

3. David Harvey, *The Condition of Postmodernity* (Oxford: Blackwell, 1989), 44.

4. Nietzsche Notebooks 1873.

5. Lars Johansson, "New Age: A Synthesis of the Premodern, Modern, and Postmodern," in *Faith and Modernity,* ed. Philip Sampson, Vinay Samuel, and Chris Sugden (Oxford: Regnum, 1984), 216.

6. Jacques-Alain Miller, ed., *The Seminar of Jacques Lacan,* book 1 trans., John Forrester (Cambridge: Cambridge University Press, 1988), 238.

7. David A. Hart, *Faith in Doubt: Non-Realism and Christian Belief* (London: Mowbray, 1993), 7.

8. Nancy A. Hewitt, "Compounding Differences," *Feminist Studies* 18, no. 2 (1992): 317.

9. Elaine Graham, *Making the Difference: Gender, Personhood, and Theology* (London: Mowbray, 1995), 185.

10. Goux, "Neutral Sex," 180.

11. D. Haraway, "Investment Strategies for the Evolving Portfolio of Primate Females," in *Body/Politics: Women and the Discourses of Science,* ed. M. Jacobus, E. Fox Keller, and S. Shuttleworth (London: Routledge, 1990), 140.

12. Luce Irigaray, ed., *Sexes et Genres a travers les langues: elements de communication sexuee* (Paris: Grasset, 1990), 13.

13. Goux, "Neutral Sex," 182.

14. Judith Halberstam and Ira Livingston, ed., *Posthuman Bodies* (Bloomington, Ind.: Indiana University Press, 1995), viii.

15. Luce Irigaray, *Marine Lover of Friedrich Nietzsche,* trans. Gillian C. Gill (New York: Columbia University Press, 1991), 118.

16. Goux, "Neutral Sex," 188.

17. Toril Moi, *Sexual/Textual Politics* (London: Routledge, 1988), 154.

18. Graham, *Making the Difference,* 173.

19. Goux, "Neutral Sex," 189.

20. Philip and Miriam Sampson, "Looking the Parts," *Third Way* 20, no. 8 (October 1997): 21–22.

21. Graham, *Making the Difference,* 173.

22. Kenneth Gergen, *The Saturated Self* (London: Basic Books, 1990), 170.

23. This is a discussion that almost takes place in Luce Irigaray, *Speculum of the Other Woman,* trans. Gillian C. Gill (Ithaca, N.Y.: Cornell University Press, 1985), 140–44.

24. Elizabeth A. Grosz, *Sexual Subversions: Three French Feminists* (Sydney: Allen and Unwin, 1989), 116.

25. See Carolyn Burke, "Irigaray through the Looking Glass," in *Engaging with Irigaray,* ed. Carolyn Burke, Naomi Schor, and Margaret Whitford (New York: Columbia University Press, 1994), 44.

138

CHAPTER 5

1. Christine Faure, "The Twilight of the Goddesses, or the Intellectual Crisis of French Feminism," trans. Lillian S. Robinson, *Signs: Journal of Women in Culture and Society* 7, no. 11 (1981): 81.

2. This may be changing with the response to Natasha Walter, ed., *On the Move: Feminism for a New Generation* (London: Virago, 1999); and Germaine Greer, *The Whole Woman* (London: Doubleday, 1999).

3. Anne and Bill Moir, *Why Men Don't Iron: The Real Science of Gender Studies* (London: HarperCollins, 1998), 21.

4. Ibid., 13.

5. Ibid., 147.

6. John Gray, *Men Are from Mars, Women Are from Venus* (New York: HarperCollins, 1994).

7. John Gray, *Mars and Venus in the Bedroom: A Guide to Lasting Romance and Passion* (New York: HarperCollins, 1995), 179.

8. Kate Fillion, *Lip Service: The Myth of Female Virtue in Love, Sex, and Friendship* (Sydney: HarperCollins, 1996), 289.

9. Garrison Keillor, *The Book of Guys* (New York: Penguin, 1994), 14.

10. Ibid., 12.

CHAPTER 6

1. Carol Gilligan, *In a Different Voice* (Cambridge: Harvard University Press, 1982); Nancy Chodorow, *The Reproduction of Mothering* (Berkeley: University of California Press, 1978); Lillian Rubin, *Just Friends: The Role of Friendship in Our Lives* (New York: Harper & Row, 1985); and Lillian Rubin, *Intimate Strangers* (Glasgow: Fontana, 1985).

2. Lynne Segal, *Slow Motion: Changing Masculinities, Changing Men* (London: Virago, 1990). See David Tacey's acknowledgment of her work in *Remaking Men: The Revolution in Masculinity* (Sydney: Viking, 1997), 9.

3. Deborah Tannen, *You Just Don't Understand: Women and Men in Conversation* (London: Virago, 1992), 14–15.

4. Ibid., 15.

5. Ibid., 16.

6. Stuart Miller, *Men and Friendship* (San Leandro, Calif.: Gateway Books, 1983).

7. Eugene Monick, *Castration and Male Rage* (Toronto: Inner City Books, 1991), 11–12.

8. Tacey, *Remaking Men,* ix, 14–15.

9. Quoted in Julia Wood and Christopher Inman, "Engendered Relations: Interaction, Caring, Power, and Responsibility in Intimacy," in *Social Context and Relationships,* ed. Steve Duck (Newbury Park, Calif.: Sage Publications, 1993), 234.

10. See Rubin, *Just Friends,* 16.

11. James Olthuis, *Keeping Our Troth* (New York: Harper & Row, 1986), 5.

12. Chodorow, *Reproduction of Mothering,* 167.

13. Gilligan, *In a Different Voice,* 8.

14. Elaine Storkey, *The Search for Intimacy* (London: Hodder & Stoughton, 1995), 197.

15. Christina Hoff Sommers, *Who Stole Feminism? How Women Have Betrayed Women* (New York: Simon and Schuster, 1994).

16. Kate Fillion, *Lip Service: The Myth of Female Virtue in Love, Sex, and Friendship* (Sydney: HarperCollins, 1996), 330–39.

17. Ibid., 17.

18. Ibid., 338.

19. Ibid.

CHAPTER 7

1. Thomas Schreiner, "The Valuable Ministries of Women in the Context of Male Leadership," in *Recovering Biblical Manhood and Womanhood,* ed. John Piper and Wayne Grudem (Wheaton: Crossway Books, 1991), 219.

2. See the discussion in Mary Evans, *Women in the Bible* (Carlisle: Paternoster, 1985); Gretchen Gabelein Hull, *Equal to Serve* (Old Tappan, N.J.: Revell, 1987).

CHAPTER 8

1. Tertullian, A.D. 160–220, *On the Apparel of Women,* book 1, chap. 1.

2. Aquinas, *Summa Theologica,* Pt 1, 4 Q xcii, art 1, 2; Q xciii, art 4.

3. Clement of Alexandria.

4. Jerome, Letter cxvii, quoted in Elaine Storkey, "Spirituality and Sexuality," in *God, Family, and Sexuality,* ed. D. Torrance (Carberry: The Handsel Press, 1996), 140.

5. Quoted by Jane Barr, "The Influence of St. Jerome on Mediaeval Attitudes towards Women," in *After Eve,* ed. Janet Martin Soskice (London: Marshall Pickering, 1990), 96.

6. William Oddie, *What Will Happen to God?* (London: SPCK, 1984), 69.

7. Ibid., 70.

8. Ibid., 33.

9. Billy Graham, "Jesus and the Liberated Woman," *Ladies' Home Journal* (December 1970), 42.

10. Alan Rekers, "Psychological Foundations for Rearing Masculine Boys and Feminine Girls," in *Recovering Biblical Manhood and Womanhood,* ed. John Piper and Wayne Grudem (Wheaton: Crossway Books, 1991), 304.

11. Raymond Ortlund, "Male-Female Equality and Male Headship," in Piper and Grudem, *Recovering Biblical Manhood and Womanhood,* 105.

12. George Knight III, "The Family and the Church: How Should Biblical Manhood and Womanhood Work Out in Practice?" in Piper and Grudem, *Recovering Biblical Manhood,* 354.

13. Mary Daly, *Beyond God the Father: Towards a Philosophy of Women's Liberation* (London: Women's Press, 1986), 133.

CHAPTER 9

1. Valerie Saiving Goldstein, "The Human Situation: A Feminine View," *Journal of Religion* 40 (1960): 100–112.

2. See Jennifer Fisher Bryant, *Lucretia Mott: A Guiding Light* (Grand Rapids: Eerdmans, 1996); and Margaret Forster, *Significant Sisters: The Grass Roots of Active Feminism 1839–1939* (Harmondsworth: Penguin, 1984).

3. A conference comment from Rosemary Radford Ruether, quoted in Letha Scanzoni and Nancy Hardesty, *All We're Meant to Be* (Grand Rapids: Eerdmans, 1992), 121.

4. Rosemary Radford Ruether, *Sexism and God-Talk: Towards a Feminist Theology* (Boston: Beacon, 1983), 111.

5. Scanzoni and Hardesty, *All We're Meant to Be,* 110.

6. Ann Loades, "Feminist Theology: A New Direction in Christian Studies," *Farmington Papers: Miscellaneous Theology* 10 (Oxford: Farmington Institute for Christian Studies, 1998), 1.

7. Phyllis Trible, *Texts of Terror: Literary-Feminist Readings of Biblical Narratives* (Philadelphia: Fortress Press, 1984), 65–91.

8. See Elizabeth Johnson, *She Who Is: The Mystery of God in Feminist Theological Discourse* (New York: Crossroad, 1992).

9. Elisabeth Schussler Fiorenza, "The Will to Choose or Reject: Continuing Our Critical Work," in *Feminist Interpretation of the Bible,* ed. Letty Russell (Oxford: Basil Blackwell, 1985), 123.

10. Ibid., 126.

11. Ibid., 128.

12. Elisabeth Schussler Fiorenza, "Roundtable Discussion: On Feminist Methodology," *Journal of Feminist Studies in Religion* 1, no. 2 (1985): 75.

13. Linda Hogan, *From Women's Experience to Feminist Theology* (Sheffield: Sheffield Academic Press, 1995), 101.

14. See the discussion of Rosemary Radford Ruether in Francis Martin, *The Feminist Question* (Grand Rapids: T & T, 1994), 178–82; and Nicholas Ansell, *The Woman Will Overcome the Warrior* (Toronto: Wedge, 1994).

15. Rosemary Radford Ruether, "Is Feminism the End of Christianity?" *Scottish Journal of Theology* 43 (1990): 390.

16. Ruether, *Sexism and God-Talk,* 12.

17. Ibid., 16.

18. Ibid., 124.

19. Ibid., 18–19. See also Pamela Dickey Young, *Feminist Theology/Christian Theology: In Search of Method* (Minneapolis: Fortress, 1990), 20.

20. Ruether, *Sexism and God-Talk,* 131.

21. Daphne Hampson, *Theology and Feminism* (Oxford: Cambridge Blackwell, 1990), 29.

22. Mary Daly, Exodus Sermon, preached in Harvard Memorial Church, 1971. See also Daly, "The Women's Movement: An Exodus Community," *Religious Education* LXVII (September–October 1972): 327–35.

23. Mary Daly, "Original Reintroduction," in *Beyond God the Father,* ed. Mary Daly (London: Women's Press, 1986), xvii, xxii.

24. Daly, *Beyond God the Father,* xvii.

25. Carter Heyward, *Touching Our Strength: The Erotic as Power and the Love of God* (San Francisco: HarperCollins, 1989), 117–18.

26. Catherine C. Kroeger, president of Christians for Biblical Equality and co-author with Richard Kroeger of *I Suffer Not a Woman: Rethinking 1 Timothy 2:11–15 in the Light of Ancient Evidence* (Grand Rapids: Baker, 1992); Gretchen Gabelein Hull, editor of the *Priscilla Papers* (St. Paul, Minn.: Christians for Biblical Equality), and author of *Equal! to Serve* (London: Scripture Union, 1992).

CHAPTER 10

1. Jean Paul Sartre, *Existentialism and Humanism*, trans. Philip Mairet (London: Methuen, 1948), 28.

2. Elaine Graham, *Making the Difference: Gender, Personhood, and Theology* (London: Mowbray, 1995), 190.

3. Francis Martin, *The Feminist Question: Feminist Theology in the Light of Christian Tradition* (Edinburgh: T & T Clark, 1994), 165.

4. Graham, *Making the Difference,* 190.

BIBLIOGRAPHY

SEX, GENDER, AND THEORY

Altmann, D. et al., eds. *Homosexuality, Which Homosexuality?* International Conference on Gay and Lesbian Studies. London: GMO Publishers, 1989.

Braidotti, Rosi. "The Ethics of Sexual Difference: The Case of Foucault and Irigaray." *Australian Feminist Studies* (1986).

———. *Patterns of Dissonance: A Study of Women in Contemporary Philosophy.* Translated by Elizabeth Guild. Cambridge: Polity, 1991.

Brown, Andrew. *The Darwin Wars: How Stupid Genes Became Selfish Gods.* London: Simon and Schuster, 1999.

Burke, Carolyn, Naomi Schor, and Margaret Whitford, eds. *Engaging with Irigaray.* New York: Columbia University Press, 1994.

Butler, Judith. *Gender Trouble: Feminism and the Subversion of Identity.* New York: Routledge, 1990.

Duck, Steve, ed. *Social Context and Relationships.* Newbury Park, Calif.: Sage Publications, 1993.

Foucault, Michel, and Jean Joseph Goux. "Irigaray vs the Utopia of the Neutral Sex." In *Engaging with Irigaray,* edited by Carolyn Burke, Naomi Schor, and Margaret Whitford. New York: Columbia University Press, 1994.

Fuss, Diana. *Essentially Speaking: Feminism, Nature, and Difference.* New York: Routledge, 1989.

———. *Inside/Out: Lesbian Theories, Gay Theories.* New York: Routledge, 1991.

Gilligan, Carol. *In a Different Voice.* Cambridge: Harvard University Press, 1982.

143

Goux, Jean Joseph. *Symbolic Economies.* Ithaca, N.Y.: Cornell University Press, 1990.

Graham, Elaine. *Making the Difference: Gender, Personhood, and Theology.* London: Mowbray, 1995.

Greer, Germaine. *The Whole Woman.* London: Doubleday, 1999.

Grosz, Elizabeth. "The Hetero and the Homo: The Sexual Ethics of Luce Irigaray." In *Engaging with Irigaray,* edited by Carolyn Burke, Naomi Schor, and Margaret Whitford. New York: Columbia Univeristy Press, 1994.

———. *Sexual Subversions: Three French Feminists.* Sydney: Allen and Unwin, 1989.

Gunew, S. *Feminism: Critique and Construct.* London: Routledge, 1992.

Halberstam, J., and I. Livingston, eds. *Posthuman Bodies.* Bloomington, Ind.: Indiana University Press, 1995.

The History of Sexuality. Vols. 1 and 2. Harmondsworth: Penguin, 1981, 1987.

Irigaray, Luce. *J'aime a toi: Esquisse d'une felicite dans l'histoire.* Paris: Grasset, 1992.

———. *Marine Lover of Frederich Nietzsche.* Translated by Gillian C. Gill. New York: Columbia University Press, 1991.

———, ed. *Sexes et Genres a travers les langues: elements de communication sexuee.* Paris: Grasset, 1990.

———. *Speculum of the Other Woman.* Translated by Gillian C. Gill. Ithaca, N.Y.: Cornell University Press, 1985.

Jacobus, M., E. Fox Keller, and S. Shuttleworth, eds. *Body/Politics: Women and the Discourses of Science.* London: Routledge, 1990.

Johansson, Lars. "New Age: A Synthesis of the Premodern, Modern, and Postmodern." In *Faith and Modernity,* edited by P. Sampson, V. Samuel, and C. Sugden. Oxford: Regnum, 1984.

Lacan, Jacques. *The Four Fundamental Concepts of Psychoanalysis.* Edited by Jacques-Alain Miller. Translated by Alan Sheridan. New York: Norton, 1978.

———. "God and the Jouissance." In *Feminine Spirituality: Jacques Lacan and the Ecole Fruedienne,* translated by J. Rose. New York: Norton, 1983.

MacCannel, J. F. *Figuring Lacan: Criticism and the Cultural Consciousness.* New York: Routledge, 1986.

Miller, Jacques-Alain, ed. *The Seminar of Jacques Lacan.* Translated by John Forrester. Cambridge: Cambridge University Press, 1988.

Moi, Toril. *Sexual/Textual Politics.* London: Routledge, 1988.

Spender, Dale, ed. *Men's Studies Modified.* Oxford: Pergamon Press, 1981.

Storkey, Alan. *Foundational Epistemologies in Consumption Theory.* Amsterdam: Free University Press, 1993.

Storkey, Elaine. "Still Moving?" *Third Way* 22, no. 4 (May 1999).

———. *What's Right with Feminism.* London: SPCK, 1985.

Tannen, Deborah. *That's Not What I Meant.* London: Virago, 1990.

———. *You Just Don't Understand: Women and Men in Conversation*. London: Virago, 1992.

Viner, Katherine. "The Personal Is Still Political." In *On the Move: Feminism for a New Generation,* edited by Natasha Walter. London: Virago, 1999.

Walter, Natasha. *The New Feminism*. London: Little Brown, 1998.

———, ed. *On the Move: Feminism for a New Generation*. London: Virago, 1999.

Wood, Julia, and Christopher Inman. "Engendered Relations: Interaction, Caring, Power, and Responsibility in Intimacy." In *Social Context and Relationships,* edited by Steve Duck. Newbury Park, Calif.: Sage Publications, 1993.

SEX, GENDER, AND SOCIETY

Ansell, Nicholas. *The Woman Will Overcome the Warrior*. Toronto: Wedge, 1994.

Arber, S., and J. Ginn. *Gender and Later Life: A Sociological Analysis of Resources and Constraints*. London: Sage, 1991.

Arnot, M., and K. Weiler. *Feminism and Social Justice in Education*. London: Falmer Press, 1993.

Bremer, C. S. "Appendix A: Women in the British Universities." In Mrs. Henry Sidwick, *The Place of University Education in the Life of Women*. London: Transactions of the Women's Institute, 1897.

Bryant, Jennifer Fisher. *Lucretia Mott: A Guiding Light*. Grand Rapids: Eerdmans, 1996.

Deem, R. *Women and Schooling*. London: Routledge, 1978.

Dex, Shirley. *The Sexual Division of Work*. Hemel Hempstead: Harvester Wheatsheaf, 1985.

———. *Women's Occupational Mobility: A Lifetime Perspective*. London: Macmillan, 1987.

Faure, Christine. "The Twilight of the Goddesses, or the Intellectual Crisis of French Feminism." Translated by Lillian S. Robinson. *Signs: Journal of Women in Culture and Society* 7 (1981).

Fénelon. *Essai philosophique sur le gouvernement civil* (1921).

Fillion, Kate. *Lip Service: The Myth of Female Virtue in Love, Sex, and Friendship*. Sydney: HarperCollins, 1996.

Firestone, Shulamith. *The Dialectic of Sex: The Case for a Feminist Revolution*. London: Jonathon Cape, 1971.

Forster, Margaret. *Significant Sisters: The Grass Roots of Active Feminism 1839–1939*. Harmondsworth: Penguin, 1984.

Glendinning, C., and J. Millar. *Women and Poverty in Britain*. 2d ed. Hemel Hempstead: Harvester Wheatsheaf, 1992.

Greer, Germaine. *Sex and Destiny: The Politics of Human Fertility.* New York: Harper & Row, 1984.

Hallett, Christine, ed. *Women and Social Policy: An Introduction.* London: Prentice Hall, 1996.

Heney, H. *Australia's Founding Mothers.* Sydney: Nelson, 1978.

Hewitt, N. A. "Compounding Differences." *Feminist Studies* 18, no. 2 (1992).

Hone, J. A. "The Movement for the Higher Education of Women in Victoria in the Later Nineteenth Century." Master's thesis, Monash, 1966.

Hooks, B., *Yearning: Race, Gender, and Cultural Politics.* Boston: South End Press, 1990.

Hubbard R. "The Emperor Doesn't Wear Any Clothes: The Impact of Feminism on Biology." In *Men's Studies Modified,* edited by Dale Spender. Oxford: Pergamon Press, 1981.

Kiddle, M. *Caroline Chisholm.* Melbourne: Melbourne University Press, 1950.

Lowe, M. "Sociobiology and Sex Differences." *Signs: Journal of Women in Culture and Society* 4 (1978).

Lowe, Marian, and Ruth Hubbard, eds. *Women's Nature: Rationalizations of Inequality.* Oxford: Pergamon Press, 1983.

Phillips, A . "Feminism, Equality, and Difference." In *Defining Women: Social Institutions and Gender Divisions,* edited by L. McDowell and R. Pringle. Cambridge: Polity Press, 1992.

Roberts, M. *Living in a Man-made World: Gender Assumptions in Modern Housing Design.* London: Routledge, 1991.

Rubin, G. "The Traffic in Women: Notes on the 'Political Economy' of Sex." In *Toward an Anthropology of Women,* edited by R. R. Reitr. New York: Monthly Review Press, 1975.

Rubin, Lillian. *Just Friends: The Role of Friendship in Our Lives.* New York: Harper & Row, 1985.

Sampson, Philip and Miriam. "Looking the Parts." *Third Way* 20, no. 8 (October 1997).

Segal, L. *Is the Future Female? Troubled Thoughts on Contemporary Feminism.* London: Virago, 1987.

Shalit, Wendy. *A Return to Modesty: Discovering the Lost Virtue.* London: Simon and Schuster, 1999.

Smith, L. T. "Maori Women, Education, and the Struggles for Mana Wahine." In *Feminism and Social Justice in Education,* edited by M. Arnot and K. Weiler. London: Falmer Press, 1993.

Storkey, Elaine. "The Same Old Story." *Third Way* 21, no. 6 (July/August 1998).

Vicinus, Martha. *Independent Women: Work and Community for Single Women 1850–1920.* London: Virago, 1985.

Waring, Marilyn. *If Women Counted: A New Feminist Economics.* London: Macmillan, 1988.

146

Weeks, Jeffrey. *Sex, Politics, and Society.* London: Longmans, 1981.

Wellings, Kaye et al. *Sexual Behaviour in Britain.* Harmondsworth: Penguin, 1995.

West, Janet. *Daughters of Freedom: A History of Women in the Australian Church.* Sutherland, Australia: Albatross Books, 1997.

Whitelegg, Marilyn et al. *The Changing Experience of Women.* Oxford: Martin Robertson, 1982.

Marriage and Family

Atkinson, David. *To Have and to Hold.* London: Collins, 1979.

Chodorow, Nancy. *The Reproduction of Mothering.* Berkeley: University of California Press, 1978.

Dominion, Jack. *Marriage: The Definitive Guide to What Makes a Marriage Work.* London: Heinemann, 1995.

Friday, Nancy. *My Mother/My Self.* London: Fontana, 1977.

Fukuyama, F. *The Great Disruption: Human Nature and the Reconstitution of Social Order.* London: Profile Books, 1999.

Gavron, Hannah. *The Captive Wife.* London: Routledge and Kegan Paul, 1966.

Hite, Shere. *The Hite Report on the Family.* London: Bloomsbury, 1995.

Oakley, Ann. *Becoming a Mother.* Oxford: Martin Robertson, 1979.

———. *From Here to Maternity.* Harmondsworth: Penguin, 1981.

———. *The Sociology of Housework.* London: Martin Robertson, 1974.

———. *Woman's Work: The Housewife, Past and Present.* New York: Pantheon, 1974.

Olthuis, James. *Keeping Our Troth.* New York: Harper & Row, 1986.

Ortlund, Raymond. "Male-Female Equality and Male Headship." In *Recovering Biblical Manhood and Womanhood,* edited by John Piper and Wayne Grudem. Wheaton: Crossway Books, 1991.

Storkey, Alan. *Marriage and Its Modern Crisis: Repairing Married Life.* London: Hodder & Stoughton, 1996.

Storkey, Elaine. *The Search for Intimacy.* London: Hodder & Stoughton, 1995.

———. "Spirituality and Sexuality." In *God, Family, and Sexuality,* edited by David Torrance. Carberry: The Handsel Press, 1997.

Masculinity

Bly, Robert. *Iron John: A Book about Men.* Reading, Pa.: Addison-Wesley, 1990.

Doty, W. *Myths of Masculinity.* New York: Crossroad, 1993.

Farrell, W. *The Myth of Male Power.* New York: Random House, 1994.

Hollis, J. *Under Saturn's Shadow.* Toronto: Inner City Books, 1989.

McCloughry, Roy. *Men and Masculinity.* London: Hodder & Stoughton, 1992.

Miller, Stuart. *Men and Friendship.* San Leandro, Calif.: Gateway Books, 1983.

Monick, Eugene. *Castration and Male Rage.* Toronto: Inner City Books, 1991.

O'Connor, Peter. *The Inner Man.* Sydney: Macmillan, 1992.

Segal, Lynne. *Slow Motion: Changing Masculinities, Changing Men.* London: Virago, 1990.

Tacey, David. *Remaking Men: The Revolution in Masculinity.* Sydney: Viking, 1997.

Tatham, Peter. *The Makings of Maleness.* London: Karnac Books, 1992.

VIOLENCE AND GENDER

Adam, Carol J. *Women Battering.* Minneapolis: Fortress, 1994.

Alsdurf, James and Phyllis. *Battered into Submission.* Downers Grove, Ill.: InterVarsity Press, 1989.

Barron, J. *Not Worth the Paper . . . ? The Effectiveness of Legal Protection for Women and Children Experiencing Domestic Violence.* Bristol: WAFE, 1990.

Bhavnaani, K. K. "Is Violence Masculine?" In *Charting the Journey: Writings by Black and Third World Women,* edited by S. Grewal et al. London: Sheba, 1990.

Hooper, C. A. *Mothers Surviving Child Sexual Abuse.* London: Routledge, 1992.

Nason-Clark, Carol. *The Battered Wife: How Christians Confront Family Violence.* Louisville: Westminster John Knox Press, 1997.

Newman, Rebecca. *Releasing the Scream.* London: Hodder & Stoughton, 1994.

Radford, J., and D. Russell, eds. *Femicide: The Politics of Woman Killing.* Buckingham: Open University Press, 1992.

Stammers, Trevor. *When Love Lies Bleeding.* London: Hodder & Stoughton, 1996.

SEX, GENDER, AND THEOLOGY

Barr, Jane. "The Influence of St. Jerome on Mediaeval Attitudes towards Women." In *After Eve,* edited by Janet Martin Soskice. London: Marshall Pickering, 1990.

Bilezikian, Gilbert. *Beyond Sex Roles: What the Bible Says about a Woman's Place in Church and Family.* Grand Rapids: Baker, 1986.

Daly, Mary. *Beyond God the Father.* London: Women's Press, 1986.

Evans, Mary. *Women in the Bible.* Carlisle: Paternoster, 1985.

Griffiths, Valerie. "Women in Mission." In *Men, Women, and God,* edited by Kathy Keay. London: Marshall Pickering, 1986.

Groothuis, Rebecca. *Good News for Women: A Biblical Picture of Gender Equality.* Grand Rapids: Baker, 1997.

Hampson, Daphne. *Theology and Feminism.* Oxford: Cambridge Blackwell, 1990.

Hart, David. *A Faith in Doubt: Non-Realism and Christian Belief.* London: Mowbray, 1993.

Hebblethwaite, Margaret. *Motherhood and God.* London: Geoffrey Chapman, 1984.

Hebblethwaite, Margaret, and Elaine Storkey. *Conversations on Christian Feminism.* London: HarperCollins, 1999.

Heyward, Carter. *Touching Our Strength: The Erotic as Power and the Love of God.* San Francisco: HarperCollins, 1989.

Hogan, Linda. *From Women's Experience to Feminist Theology.* Sheffield: Sheffield Academic Press, 1995.

Hull, Gretchen Gaebelein. *Equal to Serve: Women and Men in the Church and Home.* Old Tappan, N.J.: Revell, 1987.

Hurding, Roger. "Restoring the Image." In *Men, Women, and God,* edited by Kathy Keay. London: Marshall Pickering, 1986.

Johnson, Elizabeth. *She Who Is: The Mystery of God in Feminist Theological Discourse.* New York: Crossroad, 1992.

King, Ursula. *Faith and Praxis in a Postmodern Age.* London: Cassell, 1998.

Kroeger, Catherine, Mary Evans, and Elaine Storkey. *Study Bible for Women: The New Testament.* Grand Rapids: Baker, 1995.

Kroeger, Catherine C., and Richard Kroeger. *I Suffer Not a Woman: Rethinking 1 Timothy 2:11–15 in the Light of Ancient Evidence.* Grand Rapids: Baker, 1992.

Littauer, Florence. *Wake Up, Women! Submission Doesn't Mean Stupidity.* Dallas: Word, 1994.

Loades, Ann. "Feminist Theology: A New Direction in Christian Studies." *Farmington Papers: Miscellaneous Theology* 10. Oxford: Farmington Institute for Christian Studies, 1998.

———. *Searching for Lost Coins: Explorations in Christianity and Feminism.* London: SPCK, 1987.

Lorde, Audre. "An Open Letter to Mary Daly." In *Sister Outsider.* New York: Crossing Press, 1984.

Malcolm, Kari Torjesen. *Women at the Crossroads: A Path beyond Feminism and Traditionalism.* Downers Grove, Ill.: InterVarsity Press, 1982.

Martin, Faith. *Call Me Blessed.* Grand Rapids: Eerdmans, 1988.

Martin, Francis. *The Feminist Question: Feminist Theology in the Light of Christian Tradition.* Grand Rapids: T & T, 1994.

Mbuga, Judy. *Our Time Has Come: African Christian Women Address the Issues of Today.* Carlisle: Paternoster, 1994.

Mickelsen, Alvera, ed. *Women, Authority, and the Bible.* Downers Grove, Ill.: Inter-Varisty Press, 1986.

Perriman, Andrew. *Speaking of Women: Interpreting Paul.* London: Apollos, 1998.

Reid, John, Lesslie Newbigin, and Peter Pullinger. *Modern, Postmodern, and Christian.* Carberry: The Handsel Press, 1997.

Ruether, Rosemary Radford. *To Change the World: Christology and Cultural Criticism.* New York: Crossroad, 1981.

———. "Is Feminism the End of Christianity?" *Scottish Journal of Theology* 43 (1990).

———. *New Woman, New Earth: Sexist Ideologies and Human Liberation.* New York: The Seabury Press, 1975.

———. *Sexism and God-Talk: Towards a Feminist Theology.* Boston: Beacon, 1983.

Russell L., ed. *Feminist Interpretation of the Bible.* Oxford: Basil Blackwell, 1985.

Scanzoni, Letha, and Nancy Hardesty. *All We're Meant to Be.* Grand Rapids: Eerdmans, 1992.

Schreiner, Thomas. "The Valuable Ministries of Women in the Context of Male Leadership." In *Recovering Biblical Manhood and Womanhood,* edited by John Piper and Wayne Grudem. Wheaton: Crossway Books, 1991.

Schussler Fiorenza, Elisabeth. "Roundtable Discussion: On Feminist Methodology." *Journal of Feminist Studies in Religion* 1, no. 2 (1985).

———. "The Will to Choose or Reject: Continuing Our Critical Work." In *Feminist Interpretation of the Bible,* edited by L. Russell. Oxford: Basil Blackwell, 1985.

Sommers, Christina Hoff. *Who Stole Feminism? How Women Have Betrayed Women.* New York: Simon and Schuster, 1994.

Soskice, Janet Martin, ed. *After Eve.* London: Marshall Pickering, 1990.

Storkey, Alan. *The Meanings of Love.* Leicester: Inter-Varsity Press, 1994.

Storkey, Elaine. *Contributions to Christian Feminism.* London: Impact Publications, 1995.

———. *Magnify the Lord.* London: HarperCollins, 1997.

Stott, J. *New Issues Facing Christians Today.* London: Marshall Pickering, 1999.

Torrance, D. ed. *God, Family, and Sexuality.* Carberry: The Handsel Press, 1996.

Torrance, T. F. *The Ministry of Women.* Carberry: The Handsel Press, 1988.

Trible, Phyllis. *Texts of Terror: Literary-Feminist Readings of Biblical Narratives.* Philadelphia: Fortress Press, 1984.

Van Leeuwen, Mary Stewart. *Gender and Grace.* Leicester: Inter-Varsity Press, 1990.

Wendel, Elisabeth Moltmann, and Jurgen Moltmann. *God—His and Hers.* London: SCM, 1991.

West, Angela. *Deadly Innocence: Feminism and the Mythology of Sin.* London: Cassell, 1995.

INDEX

151

155

Elaine Storkey (D.D., Lambeth) is a sociologist and theologian of international renown. She has worked in a number of British universities and held visiting professorships in the United States. She is currently Ph.D. supervisor in theology at King's College, London; external moderator in philosophy and sociology at Birkbeck; and vice president of Cheltenham and Gloucester College. She is a regular broadcaster with the BBC, both on radio and television, and is a member of the General Synod of the Church of England and UK president of the Christian aid and development agency, Tearfund. Formerly director of the London Institute for Contemporary Christianity, she is a much published writer and the author of *What's Right with Feminism*.